The Supreme Court
and Political Freedom

The Supreme Court in American Life

Samuel Krislov, GENERAL EDITOR

The
Supreme Court
and
Political Freedom

SAMUEL KRISLOV
University of Minnesota

THE FREE PRESS, *New York*

Collier-Macmillan Limited, *London*

First Printing

To My Mother

Acknowledgments

The very title of this volume speaks of indebtedness to the work of the late Alexander Meiklejohn. Every page bears witness to this, as well as the influence of Harry Kalven, Leonard Levy, and John Roche. These men have strengthened our tradition of freedom by using free inquiry to deepen understanding of the processes of inquiry. This too has been the result of the new behavioral research on the attitudes and conduct of the mass citizenry so often ignored in most discussions of freedom of expression.

Among many obligations to my students at Minnesota and at Columbia University in 1966–67, two especially stand out—to Messrs. Theodore Pedeliski and Frank Macchiarola. My wife, Donna, took on many of the chores of authorship as often has been the case in the past. My debt to her is considerable.

Inasmuch as there is no escaping the responsibility in any event, it is merely formulistic to note that any remaining errors of fact and interpretation are, indeed, my own.

S. K.

Minnesota, August 1967

Contents

The Supreme Court
and Political Freedom

Introduction

THE ISSUE JOINED

The juxtaposition of the two principal subjects of this inquiry—freedom of expression and the Supreme Court—is both excessively familiar and passing strange. It is familiar because of the continuous and proper emphasis on minority rights in our system, on the notion that political freedom requires legal protection of organized dissent.

But the celebration of "the conventional wisdom" of our truly wise system often skirts the obvious problems and contradictions involved. Like most operating and effective organizations, the American polity is nowhere as simple as either its blind worshipers or its most avid detractors would have it. This truth is amply demonstrated in the striking fact that the heart of the democratic process, the distinctive core of our system, is defended by legal processes remote from majoritarian principles. Is this, then, as it seems, a contradiction of a most fundamental nature?

It is this basic question, which haunts almost any discussion of the Supreme Court and its role in American life, to which we will first turn and continuously return. It is in many ways a broader question still; it challenges and probes the vital relationship between professionalism and democracy, between the power of leadership and the ultimate control exercised by the common man—to critics like Ortega y Gasset, the too-common man.

The issue, too, always has a contemporary ring. Each generation faces a new form of the dilemma. The progressive era asked whether judicial opinions should not be subject to referendum and judges to recall. The depression-ridden 1930s raised the question whether economic policy should be passed on by "nine old men." Post-World War II-America pondered the issue of defining loyalty, and some thought judges (like professors) too naïve and other-worldly to intervene in a brass-knuckle world. Today, the New Left views the Court as just another committee of the establishment, just another roadblock to the true, ecstatic experience of "participatory democracy"—the good citizen's LSD.

In considering the theoretical relationship between the Court and the public, we shall discuss two general topics: (1) the differing positions of those advocating both a broad and narrow role for Court action, and (2) the empirical evidence on how the system works and how people behave. This evidence will not prove what ought to be or even all that is possible, but it will be somewhat helpful in determining what is possible.

BACK TO BEGINNINGS

From an excursion into political philosophy we shall move on to a tour of history. It will be a brief one, in full deference to Holmes' dictum that "historic continuity with the past is not a duty; it is a necessity." The heart of the Court's role in protecting freedom of expression is the First Amendment. The history of that Amendment—and, equally important, the story of how historians, jurists, and judges have viewed the Amendment—will be our second major concern.

Particularly striking is that almost all participation by the Supreme Court in civil-liberties matters is very recent. This is partly explained by the evolution of American society, partly by the passage of the Fourteenth Amendment; but mainly, the story is of the Court's progressive reinterpretation of the Constitution and its own decisions. Only an understanding of some of the peculiarities of past history makes sensible some aspects of current constitutional doctrine, although history is also often used to call into question the propriety of many a decision.

THE TROUBLE CASES

Some issues of law are relatively simple, although a good lawyer will diligently complicate them if necessary. Others present more difficult problems. At the Supreme Court level, this is not so much a matter of logic and black-letter law as it is a question of statesmanlike solutions to very difficult social problems. These solutions, difficult as they are in practical terms, are made all the more elusive because they must be justified in legal doctrine.

In recent years, a host of problems have plagued the Court and the country. Some of them, such as censorship of movies and other media, have attracted mass attention. Others, such as libel law and its developments, are rather less well-known. One of our efforts will be to delineate these problem areas.

THE IMPACT OF COURT DECISIONS

In one of Shakespeare's historical plays, a character boasts: "I can call spirits from the vasty deep." The reply is appropriate: "Why so can I, or so can any man, but will they come when you do call for them?" The question of Court logic or Court rhetoric must be secondary to the problem of what effect such injunctions have and under what conditions. This is a growing field of inquiry for scholars. But, more than that, it is a question of great practical importance: What areas of expression are most subject to Court control? Which types of official are least likely to respond to legal imperatives? Which social attitudes lead to compliance and which to resistance? In a sense, then, we shall end our inquiry as we began it, with consideration of the relationship between the Court and the public.

AN AFTERWORD FOR A FORWORD

The issues traversed here are among the most fundamental that can be raised about the American system of government. They raise problems about the moral right to govern and the nature of obligation often in dispute in these days of the sit-in and draft-card burning. They touch on the dilemma of human government suggested by Lincoln: Must a government be so weak as to permit its own downfall or so strong as to be oppressive? Our tradition asserts that there are other alternatives than these stark, undesirable ones.

But more hopeful alternatives require flexibility and calibration of solutions to new problems. The Founding Fathers could not decisively fix the course of the future with respect to freedom of expression, for, in the nature of things, they could not anticipate the practical situations to which their general principles would have to be successfully applied.

Yet, these principles are most meaningful indeed. We live in an age in which it is fashionable to denigrate democratic theory, said to be rendered obsolete by discoveries of the irrationality of man, on the one hand, and the effects of mass communication and giant industrial organizations, on the other. However, the system of pluralistic tolerance has withstood, during the past quarter-century, two rival approaches, both claiming vehemently that they were the wave of the future. Perhaps this is not accidental. The values involved in a tradition of civilized disagreement and freedom of political expression may demonstrate not only recognition of the basic human need for self-regard, as Christian Bay has argued so well, but also they seem well-nigh to have demonstrated their usefulness in terms of constructing a more viable and efficient political order.

Examination of problems in the democratic order are, of course, our prerogative in terms of our official values. But, more than that, such examination in fact strengthens and confirms the value of inquiry itself.

1

An Elite Instrumentality
of a Democratic Society

THE CONFLICT OVER
THE UNDEMOCRATIC NATURE OF THE COURT

The Constitution historically has served more
as the context for autonomous political development than as
a tight system of constraints. The wisdom of the framers, it
has aptly been said, is found as much in what was not detailed
as it is in what was specified.

Nonetheless, some matters are foreclosed, not all of
them minutiae. The states are guaranteed a republican form
of government by Article 4, Section 1; although not specified by name, the national government's basic structure is
therefore implied as well. The First Amendment also contains a series of interrelated prohibitions designed to maxi-

mize both representative government and the individual conscience.

These two basic provisions establishing the fundamental form of American government—and they are by no means the sole ones—differ from each other not only in their specificity, but also in their mode of application. The guarantee of republicanism has been a provision with indeterminate symbolic power but no legal efficacy. More specifically, the federal courts and the Supreme Court have indicated that the task of its enforcement is not theirs. The political branches of government are to enforce the spirit of this requirement. The First Amendment had a rather similar history until this century, when, by the interpretation of its words and those of the Fourteenth Amendment, it has become a major yardstick by which governmental action, both local and federal, is judged.

If a political system is to be judged by its output, civil liberties have at least been as characteristic of the twentieth-century Union as has been the development of notions of welfare. Contrary to many theoretical arguments that have been leveled, legal protection of civil liberties has been achieved in direct proportion to the expansion of the role of the government in economic matters, and the political agents of both kinds of governmental change have tended to be the same.[1]

The difference in legal enforcement of the two constitutional provisions is symbolic of even more basic cleavages

---

1. Of course, this does not logically impinge on the argument that economic freedom is functionally, not merely historically, related to political freedom. For appropriate selections by Von Hayek and others see Samuel Krislov and Lloyd Musolf, *The Politics of Regulation* (Boston: Houghton Mifflin Company, 1964), pp. 32–46. The most convincing argument—based on information costs and information loss in a system—is that of Michael Polanyi; see *The Logic of Liberty* (London: Routledge and Kegan Paul, 1951) and his discussion in Raymond Aron, *World Technology and Human Destiny* (Ann Arbor: University of Michigan Press, 1963), pp. 102–21.

among theorists, writers, lawyers, and judges concerning the role of the Supreme Court itself. To some, the emergence of Court-protected freedoms of speech, press, and assembly looms as the vindication of democratic government, a crucial intensification of the republican form of government. On this view, we can insure democracy only through the insulation of the basic machinery of free government from the temporary dangers and aberrations of majority intolerance. The issue of freedom is seen as resolved for all time, and there can be no compromise, even on a short-run basis, with threats to the basic apparatus of decision-making itself. To others—by no means necessarily less devoted to human liberty—the espousal of Court control is in itself an act of aristocratic hauteur, a dilution of the popular will. The Court, as Mr. Justice Frankfurter has observed, is after all "basically oligarchical."[2] "Courts are not representative bodies, they are not designed to be a reflex of a democratic society. This judgment is best informed, and therefore most dependable, within narrow limits."[3] Less restrained observers have gone further than that. Thus Fred Rodell has suggested, with what most would regard as hyperbole, that,

> The nine men who are the Supreme Court of the United States are at once the most powerful and the most irresponsible of all the men in the world who govern other men. Not even the bosses of the Kremlin, each held back by fear of losing his head should he ever offend his fellows, wield such loose and long-ranging and accountable-to-no-one power as do the nine or five-out-of-nine Justices who can give orders to any other governing official in the United States—from the members of a village school board who would force their young charges to salute the flag, to a President who would take over the steel industry to keep production going—and can make those orders stick.[4]

---

2. *A.F. of L.* v. *American Sash and Door*, 335 U.S. 538 (1949), p. 555.
3. *Dennis* v. *United States*, 341 U.S. 494 (1951), pp. 524-5.
4. Fred Rodell, *Nine Men* (New York: Random House, 1955) pp. 3-4.

PATTERNS OF SUPPORT AND OPPOSITION TO THE COURT

In the early history of the United States, when the Court occupied a central role, it did so as a bulwark of conservatism and a defender of property. Therefore, populist writers and their earlier counterparts could easily attack, at one and the same time, the results, the methods, and the role of the Justices with equal vigor. In an era in which Court decisions have won vital victories for populist causes—at least on paper and almost certainly in societal terms as well—a less simple state of affairs presents itself.

Some of the beneficiaries are now tempted to find new virtues in the judicial process—to assert the fundamental worthiness of judicial review and to find the Court's actions in congruence with democratic theory; others return to a less Rousseauean, more institutional base for democracy, emphasizing constitutional elements in our concept of government at the expense of populist immediacy and majoritarian control. Still others are content to take their victories where they can find them and do not feel moved to look a gift decision in the mouth. Yet others—not a few—are deeply troubled by the apparent contradiction inherent in democratic purposes being advanced through what they regard as "basically oligarchical" means.

Traditional conservative supporters of the Court have also had their problems, but economic conservatism does not preclude support for civil liberties. Indeed, tolerance of dissent and respect for due process of law tends to be positively associated with higher education and community leadership, according to studies that have been made of these phenomena, and these factors, in turn, are often correlated with economic conservatism. Thus, recent tendencies not only may not offend some of the longer-run supporters of the Court, but also may actually be genuinely welcomed by them.

However, many specific decisions of the Court—for example, the limitation on prayer in public schools and the segregation decision, for those in specific geographical areas particularly—trouble many who, by traditional group affiliation, would have been expected to be unswervingly enthusiastic about the Court. (The American Bar Association's equivocal and somewhat slow-footed support of the Supreme Court when it was under attack during the late 1950s is a case in point.) Recent economic decisions of the Court that have tended to be liberal add to these flutterings of doubt. And the product of doubts on specific results often is reflected in questioning on a theoretical level as well.

THE DEMOCRATIC DILEMMA

In part, the problem of the democratic nature of the Supreme Court—or lack thereof—is a reflection of a far-reaching and seemingly inevitable dilemma. At some point and in some way, we must define a core of democracy and insist that this core be inviolate, or else we must accept the complete and untrammeled control of the majority—the divine rule of 51 percent. To define the phenomenon of democracy, it would seem that we must assign to it some distinguishing characteristic.

The introduction of any decision rule, the mediation of an institutional pattern, in a purely logical sense alters and dilutes the "purity" of the democratic process inasmuch as it compels limitations on the majority. Yet, if there is no objective or definitional limit that we place on the concept of democracy, it has no meaning. The limitation that we suggest must exist in order to define the democratic society itself; but majoritarian control is thereby impinged upon. Since continuous ascertainment of individual will on each and every issue is impossible both practically and, probably, even theoretically, pure majoritarian control is unachievable in any event.

The further and more striking point is that, insofar as one opts for any absolute and indissoluble element as vital to the nature of democracy—and this point extends even to the minimum of requiring a majority decision—one limits the right of decision and immediate action. We cannot allow even the majority to abolish majority rule. This delimitation of democracy, the description of it as requiring some special characteristic, could thus, in a semantic sense, be called "undemocratic." Even those theorists who argue that the "democratic agreement" is procedural and by-pass the need for fundamental arguments by such concentration on machinery—on the decision rules rather than the decisions—fall afoul of this paradox insofar as they insist on any limitation on the commonweal. The quarrel on this point is not merely with the courts, but also with the Constitution and not even only with the Constitution, but also indeed with *any* constitution. This quarrel cannot be regarded as much more than puristic obfuscation, interesting enough but with little applicability. Since we cannot succeed in avoiding this contradiction, we must learn to live with it.

But, as we shall see, this objection to impediments to spontaneous action by the populace is not merely a purely logical assertion and mental exercise. It is also advanced as a programmatic element of the highly articulate and, indeed, intricately articulated philosophy of an elite group within the civil-rights movement. It therefore has important potentialities for future discussion and greater influence in the future than it has had.

DEMOCRATIC REALITIES

At present, however, a narrower antidemocratic charge is more likely to be leveled within the context of acceptance of the need for institutionalization and constitutionalism. Essentially, this argument accepts the givenness of the Constitution—the moral and historical, if not legal, commitment to a republican form of government. Within this context, institutions are judged by their own manner of operation as either partaking of or lacking democratic characteristics and contributing to—or impeding—a broader democracy.

On this less puristic test, it is also asserted, the Court fails. In this view, it would appear that the crucial discriminants are two: (1) the lack of popular involvement in the choice and/or possible removal of Court incumbents, and (2) the apparent inability of the populace to correct, modify, reward, or punish policy decisions made by the Justices except through involuted channels, extraordinary majorities required for such processes as amendment or unusually sustained majorities capable of exploiting the opportunities afforded when there occur retirement, death, or other changes of personnel. Even though these opportunities exist, however, it is clear that the sort of continuous interactive involvement that we tend to call the political process is relatively absent. A Justice once on the Court has life tenure, which, at least in part, is intended precisely to provide for insulation of the Justices from the political processes in a way that other persons in government are not.

To a certain extent, this critical evaluation can fairly be said to be mesmerized by the phenomenon of tenure and the lack of periodic election. But, in a broader sense, it is the realities of the process and not merely the narrow and singular pattern of tenure that is at issue.

The thrust of the replies to this second position tend to be thoroughly lawyerlike and, therefore, occasionally contradictory, particularly if one considers all the different authors who have chosen to reply to this claim. It is asserted with force and cogency that: (1) the Court is in every meaningful sense a participant in the political process; (2) empirically, the Court is no less responsive or democratically chosen than many other key agencies of government; (3) the isolation of the Court is appropriate and seen as democratic in the deeper sense when tested by its accomplishments and contributions to the democratic processes rather than the single—and superficial—factor of how the Justices are chosen.

Interestingly enough, then, those who criticize Court intervention are quite willing to cross swords and discuss the issue in precisely the same terms as the defenders. This has contributed to a tighter discussion than what might otherwise have ensued.

THE SUPREME COURT IN THE POLITICAL PROCESS

THE CLAIM OF COURT INVOLVEMENT

The argument that the Court is politically involved is hardly new; "th' Supreme Court follows th' illiction returns," said Mr. Dooley at the turn of the century. The current emphasis is, of course, considerably more sophisticated in technique, although, if we believe some of the lawyer-commentators on it, it is even more naïve in its conclusions.

Perhaps the most explicit statement along these lines is that of Martin Shapiro, who asserts unequivocally that the Court is not "above and beyond the political process and able to protect it impartially," as other defenders, especially Eugene V. Rostow, have claimed. Shapiro says, "If the Court is outside the process, then it is undemocratic. . . . If it is . . . outside the process then it should not make policy deci-decisions."[5] In his view it is precisely because the Court partakes of the political process that it may take a policy role:

> There is a kind of ideal type of what Courts are and ought to be . . . a type prescribing that the Judge devote his whole energy to impartially weighing the equalities and inequalities of Tom's and Joe's claim to the ownership of the horse. . . . This vision constantly interferes with a natural and unrestrained acceptance of the political role of the Supreme Court. . . . It is necessary to abandon this romantic vision in order to see that the Supreme Court is one of many multiple function agencies concerned with public law, i.e. public policy. . . . In short, the dilemma of majority and special

---

5. Martin Shapiro, "Judicial Modesty, Political Reality and Judicial Review," *Cornell Law Quarterly*, XLVII (1962), 204.

interest, power and responsibility, policy and administration, which the modest discovered when examining the Court, is not so much a dilemma as a set of outer limits within which all American government, not just the Supreme Court, operates.[6]

Shapiro does not deny that courts have their patterned behavior, their tribal customs of decision-making and decision-justifying; but these are regarded as epiphenomenal, with enduring political forces determining the matrix for what is decided, rather than these minor aspects of behavior that differentiate the judicial role from that, say, of the national legislator or city manager. Indeed, the reverse is being asserted: that which is common to all these structures is in fact controlling in by far the largest number of cases and/or largely decisive in all decisions.

The most general statement of this position, as comprehensive as Shapiro is clear and uncompromising, is to be found in the writings of A. F. Bentley. The relevance of his *Process of Government,* published after all in 1908, might seem at best tangential here except that, for more than a decade during the post-World War II era, his influence was pervasive among the behaviorally inclined political scientists and remains considerable. During the interim years, Bentley has been a force in jurisprudential thought, as witnessed by his influence on Karl Llewellyn. Bentley argued for a physics of politics—a system of analysis of the relative social power of groups whether organized or not that would enable the prediction of an outcome as the product of these confrontations. If the political order, he suggested, was properly and sensitively structured, a decision correctly reflecting underlying forces should ensue, and that decision should in turn prove stable until the balance in society shifts. On the other hand, an

---

6. Martin Shapiro, *Freedom of Speech* (New York: Prentice-Hall, Inc., 1966), p. 43.

improper decision would prove itself inadequate and unstable in short order.

This view of social policy as the vector product of underlying forces emphasizes the relative seamlessness of governmental institutions. Explicitly and implicitly, many of
those who argue for inclusion of courts under political
rubrics generally rely on Bentley. By necessity, such followers
also inherit the standard criticism made of Bentley—the
failure to properly emphasize nonmaterial influences, the
added leverage of organizational skill, and the extent to
which outcomes are affected by the structures of government
themselves. Bentley suggested that these organized groups
play an exceedingly minor role. He admitted the importance
of articulated demands; but he makes clear his basic position:

> In the societies I know most about it is my opinion—always
> subject to revision on fuller knowledge—that we already are
> able to push the analysis far enough to justify us in saying
> that the lower lying groups are affected by the discussion
> groups only in very short swings . . . that both discussion and
> organization groups yield to the lower lying groups with
> surprising rapidity when the actual change in the balance
> of pressures takes place.[7]

Contemporary research, much of it indeed influenced and
stimulated by Bentley, has seemingly and convincingly demonstrated that rather more slippage is present, that the range
of possible or reasonably adjusted decisions is considerable,
and that, in short, governments and societies are less finely
honed instruments than Bentley assumed.

In broad societal terms, viewing governmental agencies
as instruments of accommodation provides both perspective
and an analytical tool; in this abstract sense, it seems clear
that all governmental structures—the police, the professions,

---

7. A. F. Bentley, *The Process of Government* (Evanston, Ill.: The Principia
Press, 1935), pp. 445–6.

the church, the banking industry, the library, indeed all social institutions—are involved in the political process. The imperialistic meanings possible under these circumstances know no boundary, and the conceptual difficulties are almost as limitless. We are here faced with a problem similar to delineating state action under the Fourteenth Amendment, with the boundaries of that concept turning out to be increasingly difficult to construct with exactitude.

In the more precise sense of political responsiveness, the Bentley argument is perhaps relevant but even less persuasive. On this analysis, all stable governmental systems must make this adjustment, this balancing of social forces. Instrumentalities of the Soviet Union must take such an evaluation as must even the most totalitarian societies or congeries of persons, including a death camp. One may misuse Justice Black's comment on the apportionment cases here; to say that, because Courts are involved in vital decisions and their consequences, they must be reckoned to be in the political process" involves very little more than a play on words. It does not differentiate in any way between that which is and is not commonly regarded as political. It does not take into effect differences of degree in the reciprocal pressures and the relative bargaining positions of the participants. It assumes that, wherever there is any element of implicit evaluation of power, the political process is involved. It is not too much to say that all activity—and not merely all human activity— could be so subsumed.

THE REALITIES OF COURT INVOLVEMENT

But this reply is not necessarily conclusive. The Court, it is also argued, is in fact directly—not mediately, proximately, indirectly, or only analytically—involved in politics. As Von Jhering pointed out, because a judge is inviolable, it does not follow that he is inaccessible.[8]

---

8. Rudolf Von Jhering, *Law as a Means to an End*, trans. Isaac Husik. (Boston: The Boston Book Co., 1913), p. 303.

The nexus between man and men does not end up with the nomination of a judge. The publicity given to Supreme Court Justices, in fact, makes personal involvement more continuous. Robert Dahl has concluded that vacancies on the Court have recurred every twenty-two months; actually, it can be shown that, with the present-size Court, the expectation more closely approximates seventeen months.[9] A President serving two terms can precisely expect to replace a majority of members—something that he is not always in a position to do with regard to a number of quasijudicial agencies and posts. The membership of the Court itself is not fixed by constitutional means nor is it the most significant aspect of jurisdiction of the Court. These so-called "chinks in the armor of the Court" constitute opportunities for congressional and presidential influence, and they have often been exploited—although less often successfully—during key disputes in our history. Yet, their moral effectiveness as threats seems immense. The Justices are deeply conscious of the fact that they are, as Charles Curtis once put it, "a tenant at sufferance." Frank Strong more recently pointed out that current trends in constitutional interpretation can best be understood if one appreciates that, in the mind of the Justices, "the Roosevelt Court bill is far from dead," that the lessons of limited power are still fresh.[10] Similarly, Robert Dahl has concluded from the historical record that the Court has quite universally been forced to submit to pressures exerted by a national majority controlling both Congress and the Presidency. Where such power exists, the Court has succumbed in relatively short periods of time. "Nearly 30 of all invalidations have occurred after nine or more years after the initial legislation. Of those invalidated by the Court

9. Robert Dahl, "Decision Making in a Democracy: The Supreme Court as a National Policy Maker," *Journal of Public Law*, VI (1958), 279–95; Samuel Krislov, *The Supreme Court in the Political Process* (New York: The Macmillan Co., 1965), pp. 10–11.
10. Frank Strong, "Trends in Supreme Court Interpretation of Constitution and Statute," *Wayne Law Review*, VI (1960), 309.

within a four year period at least half were successfully re-implemented by congressional action."[11] The Court has indeed shown itself to be aware of the needs of group interaction and has consciously involved organized interests, at least in some small measure, in the deliberative processes of litigation. It has explicitly adjusted remedies—most clearly in equity situations—to practical exigencies and potential reaction of the populace. These and many, many more factors can be cited to indicate that traditional mythology on the role of the judge overemphasizes his uniqueness and isolation.

Throughout history, individual writers have evaluated with acumen the discretionary and social-pressure components of judgment; the uniqueness of the last half-century lies in the broad dispersion of informed speculation on the subject. The consensus of that speculation—although there are varying degrees of agreement and disagreement on specific components—suggests that judges generally, but especially Supreme Court Justices, are involved not only in the high-level statesmanship of societal accommodation, but even in the more mundane level of influence-mongering, although this involvement is still distinguishable from ward or even national day-to-day politics.

It is difficult to see, however, that this evidence fully substantiates the notion that the courts are in any adequate sense full and equal participants in the political process to the extent that they thereby acquire democratic authority or, at least, do not lose any legitimacy.

However justifiable that perspective—I would argue that no serious distortion results from perceiving the Court from a political focus—it still cannot justify extrapolating a normative justification of legitimacy that would be otherwise lacking from a political analysis of outcome. Indeed, it would appear that a truly political analysis of the Court must emphasize the extent to which it is different from, as well as

---

11. Dahl, p. 279.

like, the other branches of government, and, to this extent, it must undercut the effort to assure us that the Court is legitimized by its political activity.

THE REALITIES OF DEMOCRACY IN THE "DEMOCRATIC" BRANCHES OF GOVERNMENT

In another sense, however, Griswold, Shapiro, and others score heavily not so much in the positive justification of the Court as in the denigration of the democratic nature of other agencies of government. In so doing, however, they also add a positive perspective by suggesting that one should not view individual institutions in isolation—with the litmus of majoritarian involvement—but also by their function in the total process. We do not question the legitimacy of an administrative agency because it is appointive; neither should we foredoom the Court.

Certainly, there is some validity here. Americans naïvely have persisted in evaluating individual agencies with essential regard to their initial structure. But, on closer examination, all agencies have their cloven hoof, that is, undemocratic aspects. Specific individual units of government are adjudged, found wanting, and then entered on a dishonor roll, although, for some reason, other agencies with equal limitations are not regarded as criticizable. Thus, the Electoral College was continuously under attack decades before malapportionment, and the seniority rule in Congress seems to have attracted attention. If one analyzes the actual rules of behavior in the so-called democratic units of government, we find that they also have mixed aspects, with the possibility—sometimes the actuality—of minority control. The power of the Rules Committee, the filibuster, and the Senate are obvious shortcomings; the disequalities implicit in malapportionment, the operational consequences of seniority, and the population base of districts likely to maintain continuity in representation are more veiled aspects.

Administrative agencies hardly qualify; even their heads

are "democratically" chosen only by a certain fictional consent. The bulk of the employees are, of course, civil servants with no more than a tinge of majoritarian control. A continuum of participation rather than a dichotomy characterizes organized structures; they, in turn, must be judged by a combination of factors, including their contribution to effective government and democracy, as well as the means by which they are chosen.

Even the balance of other institutions seems relevant. Thus, the traditional bête noire of reformers—the Electoral College—assumes more acceptable connotations when it is viewed in the context of existing imbalances in the Senate and House—much as a sales tax begins to look less regressive when it is viewed in the context of new buying patterns and the less impressive progressive aspects of the income tax as actually applied.

A DIFFERENCE STILL

Although defenders of the Court score on this point, the argument is probably not as decisive as it appears on first sight. Populistic control is in fact less direct, less clearcut in the political branches than dreamt of in naïve democratic philosophy. Yet, there are differences between these branches and the Court both in the nature and intensity of the obstacles that limit majoritarian control.

These differences lie in the domain of expectancy and legitimation. Striking at the Court through "flooding the bench" by increasing the number of appointees, although constitutionally possible, proved to be a goal that eluded a President but recently elected by one of the truly historic election majorities and concomitantly with the most complete control of Congress ever granted an American political party outside the "era of good feeling." Although legal manipulation of Court numbers is possible, its use has questionable connotations, like the dissolution of the Chamber of Deputies in the Third and Fourth Republics in France. To use either the weapons of numbers or that of altering the jurisdiction of the Court for political reasons of policy differences has connotations that Joseph Rauh, the former leader of Americans for Democratic Action (ADA), once aptly although paradoxically described as "anti-constitutional though not unconstitutional." To some, such traditions of impropriety are meaningless, like verbal contracts not worth the paper they aren't written on. Yet, the same writers will generally distinguish between British government and a totalitarian order, although British rights are almost completely inherent in traditions of autolimitation and are not generally enforceable through normal legal channels.

Rebukes to administrators, to the executive power, and even to the filibuster rule do not challenge as musty a tradition or as secure an image of inviolate umpirage as critics of the Court must contend with. Specific decisions may go by the wayside—and Congress and the President have by no means been unwilling to effectively reverse Supreme Court determinations—but challenges to the basic structure of the Court power have been regarded as suspect. It is at least problematical as to who indeed won the victory of 1937. Justice (then Assistant Attorney General) Jackson put it eloquently: "The county asked, 'Is the judicial department or the will of the people supreme in America?' The Senate answered, 'Yes.' The President had said, 'let younger men constitute the judicial department.' The question was then left to another generation."[12] Indeed, the indirection involved in mounting the attack, no less than the indecisiveness of the results, suggests the relative invulnerability of the Court.

The second difference lies even more clearly in the domain of practical difficulties; the structure and role of the Court permits, although it does not guarantee, much that the independence theory accords it. The practical impossibility of involuntary replacement creates a different atmosphere

---

12. Robert Jackson, *The Struggle for Judicial Supremacy* (New York: Alfred A. Knopf, Inc., 1941), p. 155.

from that of a position at immediate sufferance. Even more significant are the transformations of role playing and role expectations. Richard Neustadt's emphasis on presidential persuasion and cajoling even within the executive branch, suggests that command situations are rare. Yet, Neustadt equally emphasizes the subtleties involved in relative power —most effective when implied rather than employed—and the leverage of moral authority that the President finds to be his greatest means of persuasion. The Court sits in consciousness and expectation of the equal and separate status conferred on it by the Constitution and history—assertion and concession.

Historians have viewed the 1937 fight and the more recent attacks in the late 1950s by Congress as proof of the Court's impotence. But, although it would hardly do to treat these as demonstrations of omnipotence, the fact remains that these efforts failed. A significant reason advanced—and who knows that it was not decisive—was indeed a functional one, a point of power. For it became clear how difficult, in fact, it was to frame legislation to "clip the wings of the Court" that did not threaten to extinguish the heart of the judicial process itself. In trying to limit the Court's authority to review limited classes of matters, Congress found itself faced with the possible evils of multiple interpretation of the law in various circuits of the country or the possibility that subject matter of unknown extent would be exempted from judicial —or federal court—review. This demonstration of the focal necessity of the Court—its combined expertise and its vital coordinating role—has been less emphasized than the sense of shock that HR3, which so soft-spoken an observer as Herman Pritchett has correctly labeled "a manifestly crackpot bill," should have come so close to final passage in 1958.[13] Yet, history must regard the failure as well as the photo finish.

And history must record also the remarkable recoveries

---

13.   C. Herman Pritchett, *Congress Versus the Supreme Court* (Minneapolis: University of Minnesota Press, 1961), p. 127.

of the Court from its two major debacles—the post-Civil War efflorescence after the Dred Scott fiasco and the post-Korean War emergence with renewed, more specialized vigor in the aftermath of the 1937 Court fight. Alone among our political institutions, the Court must cerebralize and articulate its own posture, its own contributions to the constitutional process. It has done so in our lifetime to a remarkable degree and gained from this renewed strength and a sense of its own self-worth.

All of this does not exempt it from the political process, but it does make the Court "different." And that difference may well be vital to our freedom and political survival. However much we sympathize with those applying political analysis to the Court, occasionally we must whisper with the law professors, "Vive la difference."

THE ARGUMENT OVER COURT FUNCTIONS

The argument that courts—or other political agencies—should never take on more functions than they can surely be able to cope with is more complex and less unexceptional than appears at first sight. One may well argue that, if all governmental agencies espoused that attitude, governance would become a most restricted function.

In vast areas of social interaction, government, at least nominally, undertakes to regulate matters it cannot effectively deal with. Many of these—for example, protocol with regard to individual handling of the flag—are noncontroversial, symbolic prescriptions that no one until recently seems to have thought of either enforcing or challenging. The traditional posture of the judge has perennially been Maitland's "I always stretch a statute," or the Latin tag, *boni judicis et ampliare jurisdictionem,* the legal equivalent of "a man's reach should exceed his grasp or what's a heaven for."

The usual attitude of those in enforcement positions is to build up a wide zone of possible action, permitting discretionary intervention; the policeman enforces a vast array of rules selectively, but picks an occasional target, usually after some provocation, "to throw the book at."

Courts, however, have special incentives at least to appear to reject broad swathes of authority. The extreme reliance on moral influence rather than physical or fiscal force that tends to characterize court systems, as well as the peculiar imperatives, particularly under the common law, that require them to reach a decision whenever one is properly demanded by the party, leads to an attitude of official denigration of power. So Frankfurter, then writing as the institutional historian of the Supreme Court, concluded that "perhaps the decisive factor in the history of the Supreme Court is its progressive contraction of jurisdiction."[14] But it is on the whole even more accurate to note that the culmination of this trend has been more in maximization of discretionary review than in sharp and absolute curtailment of major functions.

The theory behind discretionary review (exemplified by congressional approval of Court control over its docket through its right to grant or deny *certiorari*—in practice more than four-fifths of its caseload) was precisely that the Court could thereby define the practical limits of its own utility. This approach is hardly ministerial, and much of the argument between the so-called judicial-restraint advocates and those said to exemplify judicial activism has been in terms of the specific degree to which the Court should limit its sense of responsibility. But it must be said that there is general agreement on all sides that adjustment of effort to possible and efficient function is a source of strength for the Court. The disagreement tends to be about implementing this general principle and the extent to which it is to predominate over other factors. In a sense, it is a question as to

---

14. Felix Frankfurter and James M. Landis, *The Business of the Supreme Court* (New York: The Macmillan Co., 1928), p. 187.

whether tailor-making the Court to its possible effectiveness is merely *a* rule or *the* rule.

Judicial-restraint partisans urge a general across-the-board reticence, continuous deference when prudent, convenient, or, to their view, dictated by reason. Like their foremost spokesman, the late Justice Frankfurter, they suggest that they are often urging restraint in spite of their desire for some contrary substantive result. By implication, they suggest that their opponents are obsessed with the final outcome regardless of the means that are used. Like Philip Kurland, they are distrustful of the notion of Court omnicompetence and consider themselves members of Hand's "Society of Jobbists," who insist that the Court limit itself to those functions that it can safely, authoritatively, and pragmatically handle.

A CLOSER LOOK AT THE ACTIVISTS

The so-called activists—who in the whole reject the label —insist that "for every Justice, judicial deference is a sometime thing" and that they, too, are conscious of their roles as judges and their limitations. The activist position is by no means a stranger to abnegationist arguments. Indeed, the characterization of the Court as arrogating functions had traditionally been advanced in *criticism* of the Court's economic policies during the early twentieth century and by much the same forces that now tend to defend civil libertarians' intervention.

The activists do not reject the notion of effectiveness of Court action, but they do tend to subordinate or minimize this concept in the light of societal needs and their analysis of the nature of government, as well as the imperatives of the judicial process. Particularly, they modify the rule to suggest that what the courts can accomplish more successfully than other governmental agencies should presumptively be dealt with, if and when raised in proper legal form. So it is not merely that which the Court can be successful at, but, more precisely, that which the Court has peculiar advantage in dealing with, that becomes their test of the effective scope of the judiciary.

This position has not come easily and has been developed over time. The evolution in the thinking of the late Walton Hamilton suggests some of the patterned development of activist thought. Nor is the use of Hamilton's ideas merely of a biographical nature. He was one of the keenest critics of the "old Court" and its economic role, penning trenchant criticisms with both an analytic and historic basis. After 1937, he also devoted considerable attention to the delineation of the function and role of the Court over and above the question of particular outcomes. Hamilton and his Yale Law School colleague George Braden collaborated on a well-known article on "The Special Competence of the Supreme Court," which constructively argued that the Justices now begin to confine themselves largely to technical matters, exercising "the aloofness of self-denial." This included abjuring a broad civil-liberties role. Commenting on the position developed by Harlan Stone, they observed, "It offers no convincing argument that the protection of civil liberties lies within the distinctive jurisdiction of the Court." Nor did it, in their view, prove that "the matters at issue lie within the distinctive competence of a bench habituated to law."[15] A few years later, Hamilton was to testify before a congressional committee on judicial incompetence: "The values at stake cannot be crowded into the rigid forms of a case or controversy. The tempo is too slow for a world in a hurry."[16]

Yet, only two years later, faced with "the necessities of the case," he took a different tack. Of Justice Frankfurter, who was implementing many of the notions formerly developed by Hamilton, he observed with scorn that the Justice

15. Walton Hamilton and George Braden, "The Special Competence of the Supreme Court," *Yale Law Journal*, L (1941), 1331, 1354.
16. U.S. Congress Joint Committee on the Organization of Congress, *Hearings*, 79th Cong., 1st Sess., 1945, p. 701.

was capable only of "weaving crochet patches of legalism on the fingers of the case."[17] He heaped sarcasm on the Court's refusal to protect government employees threatened by dismissal under the loyalty program: "The Bill of Rights is too sacred to be put to so secular a use as his protection."[18] Hamilton exemplified the step-by-step development, but some other observers of constitutional problems came to this position more quickly and instinctively—notably, as we shall see, Harlan Fiske Stone.

The differentiation between more limited action in defense of property rights and greater zeal for civil liberties is hardly unique. It has been accepted, as Robert McKay points out, by every Justice sitting since 1919. Justices differ, however, in whether this difference constitutes merely a slight distinction expressed through occasional invalidation of a specific statute or action or a basic difference in the type of role to be played by the Court.

ACTIVISM AND THE CAROLENE PRODUCTS FOOTNOTE

The foundation of the activists' position is generally regarded—and on the whole properly so[19]—as found in Justice Stone's famous controversial, pithy, and cogent footnote in the Carolene Products Case. This highly reasoned statement —which belies its description by critics as framed with casualness—suggests intertwined yet disparate foundations for such a differentiated role for the Court. Each of these

---

17. Walton Hamilton, Book Review, *Yale Law Journal LVI*, (1947), 1458.
18. Hamilton, 1460.
19. In his "The Preference for Freedom," McKay suggests "preferred freedom" is a broader concept than that enunciated by Stone in the Carolene Products Case and points to the fact that, when Stone first coined the phrase in Jones *v.* Opelika, he did not tie it to the footnote. There is no doubt that the footnote is technically more narrow than the language of preference in that it deals with the question of unconstitutionality. But it seems almost ingenuous not to recognize the breadth and systematic thought that makes the footnote the source for such libertarian theory. (Robert McKay, *New York University Law Review*, XXXIV [November 1959], 1182, 1183, 1184–5.)

three notions has been continuously invoked and developed
to this day.

> *1. There may be narrower scope for operation of the pre-*
> *sumption of constitutionality when legislation appears* on
> its face *to be within a* specific prohibition *of the Constitu-*
> *tion, such as the first ten amendments are deemed equally*
> *specific when held to be embraced within the Fourteenth.*[20]

". . . We act on these matters," Justice Jackson once challenged his normal voting partner Justice Frankfurter, "not
by authority of our competence but by force of our com-
missions."[21] The job of the Court is after all to interpret
words—the words of statutes, the words of the Constitution,
the words in regulations and treaties. As Justice Black is fond
of repeating, the First Amendment is composed of rather
simple, direct, and unqualified words. Although experience
shows, in domains other than constitutional litigation, that
short, direct Anglo-Saxon monosyllables are actually more
difficult in interpretation than the highly criticized, more
flowery language of polysyllabic proliferation, this does not
free the Court from the necessity of paying attention to the
nature and structure of the injunction before them. As Black
pointed out, the First Amendment constitutes a clear and
emphatic prohibition that apparently is capable of judicial
enforcement.

There are those that disagree. Apparently following
Thayer, Learned Hand suggested that the Bill of Rights was
intended as vague, general admonitions addressed to all
branches of government, as a series of maxims intended to
inform all of their actions rather than to legally limit them.

> Indeed, these fundamental canons are not jural concepts at
> all, in the ordinary sense; and in application they turn out

20. 304 U.S. 44 (1938), n. 4.
21. *West Virginia* v. *Barnette,* 319 U.S. 624 (1943), p. 642.

to be no more than admonitions of moderation, as appears
from the varying and contradictory interpretations that the
judges themselves find it necessary to put upon them. Nor
can we leave to courts the responsibility of construing and
so of enforcing them, for the powers of courts are too limited
to reach the more controversial questions that arise under
them.[22]

He even states Thayer's cautious and doubting view of the
power of judicial review in even more extreme form: ". . . If
it [a statute] is the result of an honest effort to embody that
compromise or adjustment that will secure the widest acceptance and most avoid resentment, it is 'Due Process of
Law' and conforms to the First Amendment."[23] This peculiar
view of the Bill of Rights actually reads into the First Amendment a due process clause, even as regards national legislation. Indeed, the test is the impartiality of the legislative
inquiry, the due process of the making of the law. Hand
would thus analogize most of the Bill of Rights to the Preamble, which also is regarded as having no true independent
force. But the bulk of constitutional writers and operating
judges—and it would appear even Hand himself—have held
otherwise.

Certainly the author of the First Amendment—Madison
himself—had the possibilities of judicial enforcement called
to his attention when his correspondent Jefferson argued for
a Bill of Rights precisely because of "the legal check which it
puts in the judiciary."[24] Such writers as Ernst Freund, and
earlier writers as well, called attention to the peculiar force
of the First Amendment and its prohibitions, which were
written very much in the same style and apparently with the

22. Learned Hand, *The Spirit of Liberty* (New York: Alfred A. Knopf, Inc.,
    1960), p. 278.
23. Learned Hand, *The Bill of Rights* (Cambridge, Mass.: Harvard Uni-
    versity Press, 1958), pp. 66–7.
24. Letter from Thomas Jefferson to James Madison, March 15, 1789.

same intent as the similar prohibitions in the Constitution
itself.

> Where the makers of constitutions did intend to establish
> policies they did so in express terms: freedom of speech and
> press, religious liberty, the favor to the accused in criminal
> proceedings—these we find guaranteed in specific clauses;
> and nothing was guaranteed that had not at some time been
> a live issue. It was foreign to their minds to foreclose issues
> that no one could foresee.[25]

It remained, however, for one of the great architects of
twentieth-century constitutional liberties, Chief Justice
Hughes, to see the potentialities of the specific wording of
the First Amendment as a constitutional weapon, particularly
when distinguished from the vagueness of such concepts as
"liberty of contract." Hughes emphasized the imperative that
judges could legitimately extrapolate from such specificity.
If Black has made this position more identifiably his own, it
is because he has been more single-minded in its application
—not only in the domain of civil liberties—and even more
open and vigorous in its espousal. Yet, it was still Hughes
who originally suggested the inclusion of this clause of the
Carolene Products footnote and who must be regarded as its
immediate progenitor.

Interestingly, Louis Lusky, the law clerk whose ideas
were highly influential in developing the footnote, in later
writing on the subject was to reproduce the Carolene Products statements, but chose to omit the "express language"
argument suggested by Hughes.[26] Although pride of authorship is an obvious explanation of his somewhat bowdlerized
use of the footnote, it may well be that Lusky regards the
notion of specific enumeration as a rival theory to the

---

25. Ernst Freund, *Standards of American Legislation* (paper ed.; Chicago:
    University of Chicago Press, 1965), pp. 32–3.
26. Louis Lusky, "Minority Rights and the Public Interest," *Yale Law
    Journal,* LII (1942), 207.

political-process, minority-protection notions in the rest of the footnote. And well he might.

The promise of the protection of specifically enumerated rights is in a special sense a "jobbist" approach to the Court's role; it is itself limited and precise. But it is also essentially nondiscretionary and imperative in its implications. The Court must act when violations occur rather than choose and adjust its functions to the possibilities of the time. To those who see judicial restraint adjusted to specific situations—*ad hoc* restraint, to borrow a phrase—as the highest virtue of any judge, such compulsory activism, no matter how precisely limited, lacks appeal.

Paradoxically, it has become an activist argument, notably advanced by Justice Black, that the function of the Court is precisely determined by "orders" to it from the Constitution. The argument is that, under such a specific mandate, the Court operates safely in prescribed areas, with the maximum human objectivity, informed by history—both with regard to the adoption of the provision and its application—with clearcut legal authority, and, therefore, enhanced moral respect. Such specificity is seen as liberating the Court from the dilemma of lack of popular justification for it; indeed, it can be said to operate largely on Constitutional commission.

In short, in this view, an agency has been created with precise and limited missions. One of these is to foster the specific rights of the First Amendment. It is appropriate that the agency with this mission be insulated from political pressures; for it is precisely to overcome the daily vagaries inherent in political pressures that the First Amendment was introduced. The price of such insulation is seen as a commitment that Court intervention be, in fact, limited to matters specified as precisely as possible. The reward of the benefit is the preservation of the specific political institutions that are to be guaranteed. The watchman's role is defined so as to minimize the dangers involved in his authority, so that we need not have to exert as much energy in watching the watchman as we would in watching for the original danger that is to be avoided.

> 2. *It is unnecessary to consider now whether legislation which restricts those political processes which can ordinarily be expected to bring about repeal of undesirable legislation, is to be subjected to more exacting judicial scrutiny.*[27]

The notion of the peculiar need to keep the channels of discourse open, because impediments to free discussion prevent the self-corrective mechanisms of democracy from functioning, has been the most pervasive and appealing of all the rationales advanced for activism. Economic policies in this view can be safely left to the vagaries of an electorate that has the potential of becoming informed and that can learn of and from its mistakes. But a limit on free speech or free press simultaneously creates undesirable policies and curtails the possibility of dissemination of information about the evils of the policy. The effect of such policies are thus cumulative and often nonreversible. The hampering of opposition and criticism often becomes the vehicle for further restrictions, even to the extent of ultimate suppression. The end was forbidden by interdicting the beginnings. As the Commission of Freedom of the Press put it in 1947:

> Freedom of speech and press is close to the central meaning of all liberty. . . . Where freedom of expression exists . . . a means is at hand for every extension of liberty. Free expression is therefore *unique among liberties as protector and promoter of the others;* in evidence of this, when a regime moves toward autocracy, speech and press are among the first objects of restraint or control.[28]

The notion that the primary purpose of the First Amendment is neither ethical in origin nor an act of moral

---

27. 304 U.S. 144 (1938), n. 4.
28. Zechariah Chafee (ed.), *Government and Mass Communications* (Chicago: University of Chicago Press, 1947), p. 107.

tolerance, and even that it does not have as its purpose the achievement of social peace, but is rather basically motivated by the political needs of society has been, as we shall see, given special and convincing emphasis in the writing of Alexander Meiklejohn. It has been accepted both off the Court, by such writers as Harry Kalven, and on the bench—although with distinctive emendations—by Justices Black and Brennan. The political usage of the First Amendment lies at the root of the New York Times *v.* Sullivan decision, virtually eliminating libel suits as a consequence of criticism of public officials. That decision was hailed by Meiklejohn as, "an occasion for dancing in the streets." Although the argument for the necessity of free discussion in a democracy is hardly a novel one, it has been recreated and refurbished in our time as a central guide for American society and for the conduct of the judiciary.

This concept overlaps with the literalist approach; as Justices Black and Stone illustrate, one may hold both these notions of the basis of constitutional protection of free speech, although this is hardly compulsory. What differentiates the two is the method by which the judges' potential role is defined. The source of action is traced, in the one instance, to the wording invoked and, in the other, to philosophic inquiry into the nature of our systems and those agencies capable of meeting our needs. In the one instance, it is what the basic instruments of society necessarily command; in the other, it is what the Justices see as the commands of necessity that are to be basic.

The gulf between the political approach and that of the abnegationist tends to be rather more profound. To jobbists like Kurland, the advocates of civil liberties through the Court are obsessed with the importance of legal processes and blind to the limitations of social reality. In effect, they are accused of saying there is no salvation outside the Court. But the political-process advocates of free speech profess not to recognize themselves in this indictment; the Court does

not create the role *ex nihilo*, nor by mere fiat. It comes to it
by injunction and history. Analysis merely confirms experience and reinforces the terms under which Court intervention should be implemented. So it is no accident that
Meiklejohn relies so heavily on history in spite of the fact
that so little support can be derived from it for his thesis. As
he perhaps only instinctively understood, it is necessary to
show that it is not merely the call that the job be done that
justifies Court intervention.

Acceptance of the argument for a broader role is normally treated as a function of the Court's ability to meet the
need, but it also has the consequence—it must be noted—
that the Court looks for needs. Indeed, the libertarian position was a godsend to a deeply troubled institution unsure of
its position. Function in that sense followed need, but it is
not at all clear as to which came to rescue what.

But the political-process argument has not been without
its quandaries either. In the Flag Salute Cases, Frankfurter
took the position that, so long as the channels of change were
open, the Court had no right to intervene. Jackson rejected
this position emphatically, suggesting some rights are not
subject to the majority rule. (One is reminded of Godfrey
Cambridge's nightmare: A telephone rings and a voice announces. "We've had a referendum on slavery in California
and you lost. Report to the auction block in four hours.")
But Frankfurter's argument itself pinpoints its own refuta-
tion: Most restrictions on liberty are not overtly handicaps to
seeking remedies to that specific legislation. To take another
instance, the Communists were free to seek repeal of the
Smith Act.

Truly subtle judgments are involved in evaluation of the
degree to which a law operatively or, by attaching a stigma
to a group, in effect carries with it a perpetuation of its own
repressiveness. It is revealing that Frankfurter himself seldom
if ever found clogging the channels of political change to be
sufficiently present to cause him to advocate invalidation of

legislation.[29] In short, the political process argument inadequately justifies the domain of liberty normally sought by activists; and inasmuch as the third notion of the Carolene footnote—the "enclaved-minorities argument"—rests to some extent on political-process concepts, Hughes' judgment on including an argument from specificity of language seems to have been vindicated.

Indeed the political-process argument is quite capable of being employed as an antilibertarian argument, as Willmoore Kendall has demonstrated. Virtually paraphrasing—if not burlesquing—Meiklejohn, Kendall has argued that the process of discussion itself often requires curtailment of debate, even employing Meiklejohn's town-meeting model to derive his indictment of the open society.[30]

The attractiveness of the political argument—in essence a social utilitarian rationale for expression, rather than an individualist ethical one—are many. But it appears that it does not capture all the essence of the former notions of liberty. Indeed, not only has there been need to buttress the political-process argument with other, more individualist arguments also stemming from John Stuart Mill, but also there has been felt a need to express separately and uniquely the older ethical concept of self-fulfillment—formerly viewed as

29. Wallace Mendelson, "On the Meaning of the First Amendment: Absolutes in the Balance," *California Law Review,* L [1962], 824), takes Frankfurter's statement in Barnette at face value, as a statement of his fundamental position. But in both Douds and Dennis the Justice, with admirable frankness, noted that curtailment of liberty was present, yet he found this overbalanced by other considerations, so that *even* curtailment of remedies was not sufficient to require unconstitutionality. The curious fact about Frankfurter's judicial heritage is that he has left elaborate justifications of judicial inaction, but has left blurred and unrationalized his positive exercise of judicial power —as for example, in the School Prayer Cases, or (even though with some efforts at conceptualization) the Commerce Clause Cases. In view of his fundamental distrust of Court power, it would appear to have been part of the need to redefine judicial review positively as well as negatively.

30. Willmoore Kendall, "Do We Want an Open Society?" *National Review* (January 31, 1959), 491–3.

the source of libertarianism—in the legal notion of privacy. Even on social utilitarian grounds, Henry Steele Commager has urged what he suggests is a firmer basis for a broad libertarian doctrine, "the material value of independence of thought."[31]

> *3. Nor need we inquire whether similar considerations enter into the review of statutes directed at particular religions . . . or national . . . or racial minorities . . . whether prejudice against discrete and insular minorities may be a special condition which tend seriously to curtail the operation of those political processes ordinarily to be relied upon to protect minorities and which may call for correspondingly more searching judicial inquiry.[32]*

The final—and also appealing—suggestion of Stone was that those groups that could not use the political processes effectively to present their points of view should therefore be accorded Court protection. Again, this notion is closely compatible with the exact wording of the Constitution—particularly the requirements of the Fourteenth Amendment for equal protection—and can be regarded as a natural partner to Hughes' "specific wording" notions. The basic idea is derived from an unexpected source—Marshall's opinion in the National Bank Case, McCulloch v. Maryland. Marshall had suggested that the national government was entitled to tax immunity from the state whereas instrumentalities of the state could be taxed by the national government. The reasoning was that a state could enrich itself at the expense of the nation, but the nation, composed of fifty states, would and could not so abuse itself. The national government did not otherwise have the means to reverse a decision within the

---

31. Henry Steele Commager, "The Pragmatic Necessity for Freedom," in Clair Wilcox (ed.), *Civil Liberty Under Attack* (Philadelphia: University of Pennsylvania Press 1951), p. 8.

32. 304 U.S. 144 (1938), n. 4.

locale of a state, but a national provision could be reversed by the considered actions of the states harmed by the action.

In analogy with this, the Carolene Products footnotes suggests that only certain kinds of minorities—"discrete and insular ones"—are to be accorded special judicial protection. Presumably, it would be in light of minority inability to communicate generally with the electorate that the Court would act.

There are several difficulties with this concept that have never been resolved. To decide which minorities to single out in our society for such judicial concern is not always easy. Certainly, from a political-process standpoint, any group that is outvoted can be regarded as a minority, and it is not at all clear when its situation becomes insular—"enclaved"—and when its actions are merely the normal problems engendered by a minority being unable to convince the majority.

Disqualification on the basis of race and previous servitude is specifically outlawed by the Constitution and thus is indeed judicially protected. But this last clause of the Carolene footnote would appear to be an independent concept justifying a differential role that presumably would not necessarily be bounded by the categories found in the rest of the Constitution. Why the wealthy do not constitute an insular minority, or Republicans in Tennessee—who are indeed geographically isolated—or city dwellers in a rural state, or ruralities in a metropolitan-controlled political jurisdiction is not necessarily clear. Extending this argument, Martin Shapiro has argued that the Court ought to keep a jealous eye out for precisely the groups who are not properly represented by the political process for one reason or another.[33] The exact dimensions and intensity of intervention would depend not only on the degree of insularity, but also, presumably, on the logic of their case.

It is, of course, clear that, if the Court should indeed

---

33. See Shapiro, *Freedom of Speech.*

represent those forces that are significant in our society but for some reason are cut off from the political process, then it is both logical and mete that the Court should not come immediately under the control of any organized majoritarian control. But if migratory workers are normally unable to convey their point of view, not because of lack of numbers, but because of the nature of their lives, their pattern of residence and leisure time, the Court might assume some greater protectiveness toward them not merely as an expression of what Morely called "infracanineophilism" (or, a love of the underdog), but as a healthy expression of the need for society to properly correct some of the inequities that are inherent in any institutionalization of the political process. The Court is not seen merely as the conscience of the nation, but also as the agency of government that is relatively free from immediate day-to-day pressures and thus as the one that represents future balances as well as those of the present. Presumably, if the balance struck by the Court is an improper one, then the political branches of government would be able to assert their sway. In this concept, such action as reapportionment, which attempted to restore political control to a numerical majority was justifiable, and it is perhaps not a coincidence that it is this Court action of all those of recent years that has been the most sharply and consistently criticized by abnegationists.

THE COURT AND POPULAR SUPPORT
FOR LIBERTY

Prescription does not always follow from description; that which is cannot legitimately presume to dictate all that which we believe ought to be. Yet, empirical findings of existential relations are hardly irrelevant. In the dissection of the nature of democratic participation evidence has been amassed, in recent years, that must inform our sense of how individuals operate within a political system. As in most situations, this evidence is not without its ambiguous application; yet, the advocates of a strong Supreme Court role can fairly claim that our growing, although limited, knowledge of political man suggests the importance of structural support for democracy and encourages more extensive utilization of legitimating structures and symbols in defense of liberty.

Modern evidence seems most consistent with the concept that democratic ideals are generally remote from the day-to-day thought processes of the common man who intuitively and temperamentally is neither generous nor tolerant. In general, the common man is indeed little involved in the participatory process. Even in the field of religion, commonly thought to be a lower-class phenomenon, evidence now indicates that participation is more common at the middle- and upper-class levels. (Even participation in fundamentalist religious groups is more commonly found among upper-class individuals, although, within the population that involves itself in religion, a higher percentage of working-class individuals prefer a fundamentalist approach.)[34] Not only is participation not likely to be broadly dispersed, but also social attitudes are relatively concentrated. Although prosperity and broad distribution of education, information, and material means are conducive to a democratic atmosphere, they hardly guarantee it. The evidence seems strong that the basic modes of societal operation and the values and methods of conduct of leadership groups are ingredients that can strongly modify and mitigate mass opinion most profoundly; it suggests that democratic values radiate not from the masses to the leadership, but rather from the leadership to the general community.

Thus, the structures by which group demands are articulated and the responses of leaders become key elements not

---

34. Charles Y. Glock and Rodney Stark, *Religion and Society in Tension*, (Chicago: Rand McNally & Co., 1965) chaps. x–xi; see also Murray Hausknecht, *The Joiners*, (New York: Bedminster Press, 1962).

only in determining the actual outcome, but also in affecting the attitude of the populace as to the proper means for assertions of demand and the way to proceed in considering those demands. (The parallelism here to the reasoning in the Carolene Products footnote on the special need to protect the democratic process is seemingly coincidental but suggestive.) Furthermore, there is evidence that actions taken by such an authoritative agency as the Court have consequences in popular opinion on the substantive issues as well. Positive action by legitimating agencies itself tends to breed support or discourage adherence to a policy or value.

Overwhelming evidence has accumulated of the marginal—at best—interest in political events. The fact that for the bulk of voters participation is neither a highly informed nor a highly valued action has led some to feel a conflict between alleged faith in human rationality in policy-making —supposedly inherent in democratic theory—and the demonstration of the seemingly irrelevant factors actually involved in the decision process for the average voter. To others, however, these findings suggest a firmer and closer basis precisely for classical democratic theory and its institutionalist–constitutionalist–pluralist balance of power notion, which emphasizes the need for multiple foci of power, with healthy skepticism about majoritarian control. Embracing Reinhold Niebuhr's view that man's corruptibility defines the gingerly relationship of ruler and ruled, with checks needed in both regards, such an approach is not undermined by the limitations of the average man but sees no point in glorifying him. The essence of this position is fairly well captured by Churchill's observation that democracy is a very bad form of government that is merely the superior one of all men have experienced.

It has been a commonplace to suggest that classical liberal democratic theory has been undermined by such findings, and at best all that can be preserved of that ideology is its function as a Platonic or Sorelian myth. But, on the specific issue of constitutional law and civil liberties, the general public's level of information is even more singularly unimpressive. Attempts to raise that level of information—as in the Fund for Republic's expenditure of effort and money for a "Freedom Agenda" campaign—have had no apparent effect.

Insistence that the tradition of civil liberties can best be appreciated only by the inheritors of nineteenth-century genteel liberalism—that freedom of speech is caviar to the multitude—is, in a certain sense, highly realistic, as studies have continued to show. But it leaves one open to a curious charge of inconsistency and lack of confidence in the very people who are supposed to be enlightened by the process of free communication at issue. It raises the question of the meaning of a "tradition" that is upheld by practically no one. And, in a larger sense, it is unrealistic in that ultimately elite opinion has been demonstrably responsive to mass reaction and peculiarly nonresistant to what appears to be overwhelming sentiment. Ultimately, freedom of speech clearly rests on at least tolerance by the majority, as well as espousal by a minority.

Even more significant than the level of information—invincible ignorance is after all excused—is the level of support for civil liberties. In the rhetoric of libertarianism, it is the bad ruler who sets out to deny liberty in the face of the protests of the majority. "Power tends to corrupt and absolute power corrupts absolutely." But the American public emerges as profoundly indifferent to liberties long established and presumably noncontroversial. Indeed, a reviewer of Samuel Stouffer's *Communism, Conformity and Civil Liberties,* the most extensive survey of popular attitudes ever taken among the general public, was prompted to conclude that even Senator Joseph McCarthy or the leaders of the Daughters of the American Revolution would have to be accounted libertarians in contrast to the attitude of the general public.[35]

---

35. Nathan Glazer, "Civil Liberties and the American People," *Commentary,* XX (August, 1955), 169.

Over the years, a series of carefully structured studies, surveys, and polls, as well as assorted grab-bag questionnaire arrangements ascertaining the views of groups of questionable representatives, all have probed and examined the attitudes of Americans toward civil liberties. Apparently without exception, these studies record profound antilibertarianism latent throughout our society.

This emerges as a paradox of no mean proportions. In the first instance, when asked to speak in terms of broad values, Americans consistently wrap themselves in the libertarian mantle. Americans overwhelmingly favor civil liberties when asked about their attitudes in highly abstract terms. However, when queried in operational terms, without benefit of shibboleths to guide them, they give antilibertarian responses about rights that are disputed. Many, if not most of these the same liberties they support in the abstract. Yet, in practice, Americans seem to provide sufficiently broad general support for such rights to sustain them against attacks on a legal and practical level. This three-tiered pattern of response seems constant, clearcut, and highly significant in all of its aspects. It would appear to be a fact of American political life that all three levels of response are interdependent and significant.

The contradiction between broad libertarian sloganizing and more concrete antirights attitudes can be taken as a devasting indictment of democracy and as a sign of the irrelevance of the most general articulated values. But this is probably an error; the fact that "all declare for freedom but proceed to disagree as to its application" permits the final outcome or resolution in favor of the disputed rights in practice when the decision emerges, after being channeled through prescribed structures. In short, this means that the discrepancies between highly abstract values and concrete principles can be exploited effectively by those in a position to work for the asserted rights in practice.

The antilibertarian impulse of the general American

public, specifically working-class respondents, seems well established, as does the general class bias in libertarian attitudes. Libertarianism emerges largely as a middle- and upper-class luxury. For example, some studies show Republicans more libertarian than Democrats—presumably because of the high working-class components in the latter party—in spite of the fact that the Democrats as a party have taken many more stands favorable to civil liberties. Despite this working-class bias against libertarianism and evidence that education is positively correlated with libertarian views, it is instructive to note that it is on the basis of study of the attitudes of college students—a group strongly skewed on both class and education levels *toward* libertarianism—that some sociologists and political scientists have concluded that the Bill of Rights would be rejected by the populace if it were up for adoption today.[36] Even college students as a group seem lukewarm to liberty.

Some indication of this lack of libertarianism can be gleaned from the results of a group of questions given as part of Stouffer's study of anti-Communist reactions by the public. Public attitudes were tapped in 1954, at a time when repressiveness was at a comparative high point in American history. Although studies show variations between regions in degree of support for the Bill of Rights, with a consistent pattern of much more support in the West and the East—a pattern that is consistent on all kinds of issues—no region emerges with a majority as libertarian as current judicial decisions.[37]

36. See, for example, Hanan C. Selvin and Warren O. Hagstrom, "Determinants of Support for Civil Liberties," *British Journal of Sociology*, LI (March, 1960), 51–73; and Raymond Mack, "Do We Really Believe in the Bill of Rights," *Social Problems*, III (1956), 264.

37. Some useful summaries of data on these points include, Herbert Hyman and Paul Sheatsley, "Trends in Public Opinion on Civil Liberties," *Journal of Social Issues* IX, (1953), No. 6; Hazel G. Erskine, "The Polls: Some Gauges of Conservatism," *Public Opinion Quarterly* XXVIII (1964), 154; Hadley Cantril and Mildred Strunk, *Public Opinion 1935–1946* (Princeton, N.J.: Princeton University Press, 1952).

The continued class difference in general tolerance of dissent has also been shown so consistently as to lead to the coining of the expression "working-class authoritarianism" to suggest that liberties are most secure with the upper-class. In recent years, the most conspicuous leaders of American social science have had an anti-working-class and pro-elite orientation in their prescriptions on the export of democracy. The circumstances under which these notions gained ascendancy —the period of McCarthyism, with its concomitant estrangement of intellectuals from mass opinion and the shift in the social standing of intellectuals in an upward mobile fashion —are, of course, suggestive and make such findings somewhat suspect. But even before these elitist notions gained general currency, they constituted the operational code of the American Civil Liberties Union—always a national-office operation viewed as an elite-centered negotiating group—and figured in the analysis of keen observers of our society. Furthermore, the almost unprecedented consistency in the pattern of responses over other eras is also impressive, including years prior to the period in which these notions became fashionable among social scientists.

No different attitude emerges on issues not involving communism; indeed, atheist speech seems the most controversial (see Table 1–1).

Table 1–1—Attitudes of Community Leaders and General Public Toward Selected Free-Speech Issues

ISSUE: PERMITTING SPEECHES	COMMUNITY LEADERS			NATIONAL CROSS-SECTION		
	Yes	No	Und.	Yes	No	Und.
Advocating government ownership of industry	84	14	2	58	31	11
Against churches and religion	64	43	2	37	60	3
By a person accused of communism who denies it	87	11	2	70	21	9
By an admitted communist	51	47	2	27	68	5

Source: Samuel Stouffer, *Communism, Conformity and Civil Liberties* (New York: Doubleday & Company, Inc., 1955), pp. 29, 33, 36, 41.

The Stouffer study also can be placed in the context of trends in public-opinion polls both before and since it was published. Although there have been significant increases in support for liberty on a number of issues, it is even more significant that so large a percentage of the populace, and even of leaders, support bans that are so far from constitutional doctrine the cases would almost certainly never get to the Supreme Court. When CBS ran its first National Citizenship Test a few years ago, a majority of *Congressmen* answered its free-speech question incorrectly; only a small minority of the general public had an accurate view of legal doctrine. A sophisticated study of young peoples' attitudes—based on an admittedly small sample—found only 25 percent in agreement with Supreme Court doctrine on free speech and assembly and only 10 percent with free-press decisions!

It has been suggested that the class-bias conclusions drawn from the data is due to class-based differences in propensity to disagree with items and opinions. Evidence has indeed been accumulated to suggest that lower-class and less well-educated persons have a lesser sense of personal efficacy and more of a tendency to accept at face value statements given to them to answer "yes" to any statement. On the other hand, education usually encourages closer examination of and more frequent disagreement with items. This problem of the "response set" of questions usually has not been faced squarely by researchers in the Bill of Rights areas, although it can be dealt with in part by varying the language in individual items so that both positive and negative items appear. Response set, however, is not an obstacle to generalization in this instance, for it happens that, apparently inadvertently, some researchers have listed their questions in negative terms; that is to say, the antilibertarian items in some studies required contradiction of the original item and in others merely affirmation of the item. Comparing the two different types of situations does not, in fact, suggest that the results obtained about attitudes toward civil liberties are spurious.

Indeed, the class bias emerges as much from the one type

of question as from the other, suggesting that, when we are dealing with such matters as rights of the accused and the like, attitudes are sufficiently congealed so that agreement is readily tapped.

In recent years, more sophisticated studies—such as the McCloskey study (Table 1–2)—do control for acquiescence set and confirm earlier findings.

Table 1–2—General Principles and Specific Applications: Responses of Influentials and the General Electorate (1957)

General*	% Influentials	% General Electorate†
People who hate our way of life should still be heard	86.9	81.8
I believe in free speech for all	89.4	88.9
You can't know truth unless opposite views are free	94.9	90.8
Applications		
Freedom doesn't entail right to teach foreign ideas	45.5	56.7
A book with wrong political ideas can't be good	17.9	50.3
In dealing with dangerous enemies we shouldn't rely upon slow methods of court and law	7.4	25.5

* Items abbreviated.

† Only agreement figures given in original study, as "no opinions" were negligible.
Source: Herbert McCloskly, "Consensus and Ideology in American Politics," *American Political Science Review*, LVIII (1964), 361, Tables II, III.

The most interesting and influential finding of the Stouffer study generally cited, confirmed by such efforts as the Selvin-Hagstorm and the McClosky studies, has been the discovery that community leaders were vastly more tolerant than the general population. Even those organizations who were dedicated to repressive programs with regard to civil liberties in the McCarthy era were led by individuals distinctly more libertarian than the mass population. The conclusion is that leadership itself requires or encourages more tolerant attitudes. The difficulty with this finding is that the Stouffer study does not help us to determine whether it is as a result of their activities that leaders appreciate tolerant attitudes or it is the selection process that determines that people with such values are chosen—or that attracts such personality types. It seems clear that the leadership function is associated with more tolerance, even controlling for education and class levels (although even that does not decisively emerge from the Stouffer data). What is not clear is whether it is the selection process or the leadership process that produces such values.

Recent advocates of greater participatory democracy— notably the New Left civil-rights groups—argue that dispersion of leadership functions and encouragement of greater participation on the part of the mass public will lead to more libertarian attitudes, as apparently the process does for community leaders. This would be true, of course, only if it is indeed the process of leadership that produces libertarians and not merely the selection process that finds them.

In any event, there are also significant practical problems involved in dispersion of leadership throughout a population; perhaps the most obvious cost is the vast increase in social time necessary to carry on decision-making in such a society. Our knowledge of organizations suggests that such efforts are utopian in the best sense of the word, and evidence suggests that true mass decision-making tends to be a temporary phenomenon and a particular function of a particular time and need. (There are both demographic and psychological reasons limiting dispersal of leadership functions throughout a group. Assuming a rather fixed ratio of leadership functions in any society—beyond which dispersion of the functions would become inefficient in the extreme—it would appear that, with a large population, an increase in births would tend to out-distance the possible maximum rotation of individuals.) In any event, it is important to note that studies, even of organizations devoted to dispersion of leadership, have confirmed at least some of the milder forms of the iron law of oligarchy.

The more common reading of the Stouffer study, however, has simply emphasized the importance of heeding authoritative positions in defending civil liberties. Looking about the world, for example, Herbert Hyman has concluded that antilibertarian attitudes tend to be the reflex action of the mass population everywhere. Thus, it is doubtful that the general population in Great Britain has a more favorable attitude toward civil liberties than do Americans, as is sometimes alleged. In Australia, Hyman notes that poll results before and after a referendum on the banning of the Communist Party favored such a ban, but the actual vote was against repression. He suggests that it is likely that there, as in the United States, opinion refined through institutional and leadership structures is more likely to be tolerant than off-hand expression of attitudes in response to casual questions.[38]

The evidence is strong that an enactment of a law by Congress results in a higher level of approval of the measures so passed. A winning candidate for President has a higher majority in the memories of people who thought they voted for him than his actual recorded vote. A Supreme Court decision influences popular opinion and gives moral stature to the person who acts in its name. The very emergence of a militant civil-rights movement is one case in point. Equally significant is the reaction of mobs who, after the Gobitis decision requiring school children to salute the flag, attacked Jehovah's Witnesses Headquarters with the shout, "The Supreme Court is with us."[39] When the Attorney General condemned the DuBois clubs, a series of bombings and attacks developed.

The stuff of authoritativeness, the label of legitimacy that is sought for all governmental policies and indeed constitutes its primary possibility of acceptance, radiates beyond the measures of the law. Indeed, the concepts of "authority" and "legitimacy" necessarily involve symbolic and irrational

38. Herbert Hyman, "England and America: Climates of Tolerance and Intolerance," in Daniel Bell (ed.), *The Radical Right* (New York: Anchor Books, 1964), pp. 269 *ff.*
39. F. H. Heller, "A Turning Point for Religious Liberty," *Virginia Law Review*, XXIX (1943), 449. These attacks were cited as a basis for decision in *Busey* v. *D.C.* 13 F. 2d (1943), p. 595 n. 21.

elements over and above their utilitarian components. People do not obey the law only because of very careful utilitarian analyses, even though the habit of obedience may well be based in very broad terms on social utilitarianism. It is clear that symbolic overtones of authoritative decisions carry consequences beyond the narrow action involved. Thus an action of the Court dealing with a specific civil-liberties issue has connotations beyond that issue and authoritatively suggests that defense of other liberties makes sense as well. Refusal to deal with a problem is usually viewed as rejection of liberty or, at least, its minimization. It is not merely viewed as a question of authority, responsibility, or separation of powers.

While conceding that, in fact, in American politics, this is the situation today—that Court action or inaction is taken as a symbol of the desirability and importance of the issue involved rather than as a legal question of power and jurisdiction—critics of an expansionary role for the courts and civil liberties have argued that this is indeed the heart of the problem. By judicialization of such matters, they take them from the arena of popular responsibility and suggest to the general public that they are matters that can be left to the courts. Thus, in his "tribute" to the late Mr. Justice Rutledge, Wallace Mendelson rather bitterly observed that:

> While he could not always follow the logic of his position, in the log of history, Rutledge's name must be associated with the preferred place doctrine—that *beau geste* which would give Americans better government than they are. at the moment able to give themselves and take from them (perhaps merely dilute) moral responsibility for their acts which is the indispensible matrix of human freedom.[40]

Similarly, it is argued that, in Great Britain, the general public is more alert and responsive to violations precisely

---

40. Wallace Mendelson, "Mr. Justice Rutledge's Mark upon the Bill of Rights," *Columbia Law Review*, L (1955), 51.

because it does not have a "let Justice George do it" attitude. The late Justice Jackson, for example, suggested that,

> In Great Britain, to observe civil liberties is good politics and to transgress the rights of the individual or the minority is bad politics. In the United States, I cannot say that this is so. Whether the political conscience is relieved because the responsibility here is made largely a legal one, I cannot say, but . . . I do not think the American public is enlightened on this subject.[41]

In part, statements about the pre-eminence of politics as defender of British liberty are based on appearances. In his preface to Dicey's authoritative *The Law and the Constitution,* Professor E. C. S. Wade offered the following proposition:

> It is only, where constitutional law is concerned, in that small but vital sphere where liberty of person and of speech are guarded that it means the rule of common law. For here alone has Parliament seen fit to leave the law substantially unaltered and to leave the protection of the freedom of individuals to the operation of the common law.[42]

Nonetheless, the ultimate, even if only occasionally exercised, authority is clearly political, so that the thrust of Justice Jackson's remarks may be deflected but not avoided. In direct response to Jackson, the legal philosopher Edmond Cahn observed that such advocates wanted to import a part of the British system—that part weakening civil liberties—without the supports for liberty implicit in the centralized governmental structure that could control the localities. Perhaps even more significantly absent is a political structure

---

41. Robert Jackson, *The Supreme Court in the American System of Government* (Cambridge, Mass.: Harvard University Press, 1955), pp. 81–2.
42. E. C. S. Wade, Preface to A. V. Dicey, *The Law and the Constitution* (9th ed.; London: Macmillan and Co. 1939), p. lxxii.

that involves party responsibility and national responsible leadership. The evidence would suggest that not only would it require a political system of the parliamentary type as Cahn suggested, but also the importation of something more nearly approaching the British social order as well.[43] In short, it is the more tightly focused elite leadership of all aspects of British life that permits focus on liberty rather than the type of broad popular support suggested in the Frankfurter–Jackson–Mendelson thesis. There is no compelling evidence —and indeed some highly negative information—that the British public generally—as opposed to its activists and attentive public—are more libertarian than Americans.

Furthermore, as Laurent Frantz reminds us, Frankfurter and his followers have not advocated a system with no judicial review, or even one without review based on the Bill of Rights. (The latter position has been advocated only and sporadically by Learned Hand and perhaps by Henry Steele Commager.) Rather, they speak of minimization of the judicial role, so that the Court would continue to pass on restrictive legislation but virtually never do anything but validate legislation. This, he argues cogently, is the worst of all possible constitutional worlds—the fact of legislative omnipotence would be concealed and the imprimatur of Court evaluation somewhat fraudulently added.[44]

In this view then, Court inaction is not merely a neutralist position. It would amount to an antiliberty stand. As long as the Court survives, it must act one way or another. The removal of Court authority from the domain of civil liberties or its minimization will not therefore contribute to greater democratization of the society without far-reaching changes in American political life and the American charter —changes we have no reason to expect. On the other hand, the removal of the symbolic authority of the Court for specific

43.   Edmond Cahn, *Can the Supreme Court Defend Civil Liberties?* (New York: The Sidney Hillman Foundation, n.d., Pamphlet No. 9).
44.   Laurent Frantz, "Is the First Amendment Law?—A Reply to Professor Mendelson," *California Law Review*, LI (1963), 744.

means and programs will have repercussions far beyond those matters narrowly at stake before the Court.

CONCLUSIONS

Edwin Corwin once shrewdly observed that judicial review is "American democracy's attempt to hedge its bet."

In recent years, such writers as Charles Black, Griswold, Rostow, and Shapiro have attempted to redeem the Court and to suggest that its authority is at least not antidemocratic. Adherents of this antiantidemocratic position have successfully made a number of points about the nature of political institutions and the nature of participation in the political process. Basically, they have shown that all political agencies have aspects of their operations that only in some ultimate sense are reconcilable with majoritarian rule. They also rely heavily on social-science studies indicating that mass participation is somewhat illusory and that, in addition to rationalistic considerations, symbolic and authoritative factors necessarily operate in a political order, at least in the short run. They have also argued that the Court is indeed involved in the political process and is subject to some ultimate control. It is suggested here that this does not fully justify the case for regarding the Court as on all fours with Congress and the Presidency, even though some of the notions of popular control of those institutions are readily demonstrated to be naïve. In this respect, we have warned against oversophistication as well as oversimplification, emphasizing some of the differences that must be acknowledged. Indeed, it has been suggested that such controls—such as the possibility of flooding the Court and changing the jurisdiction of the judiciary —are highly desirable weapons, particularly if never used. Further, the argument for complete insulation of the Court should be rejected precisely because of the differences between the branches of government and the paradoxical need for maintaining similarity through political controls.

Liberty in the Views of Historians and the Works of Judges

PERSONAL INVOLVEMENT AND THE HISTORIANS OF LIBERTY

The history of the First Amendment has been written in much the same spirit as that in which Samuel Johnson recorded parliamentary debates. He told the truth, he noted, but took "good care to see that the Whig dogs did not get the better of the argument." The Founding Fathers, it appears, were libertarian, legalistic, conservative, or zealous largely in the image of the chronicler—much as we are told that English experimental psychologists observe matter-of-fact, pragmatic rats; Americans observe bustling rats; and Germans see copiously organized rats. The issues of freedom seem to touch a highly personal nerve, so that one tends to bring to the issue an enormously convincing viewpoint under which the facts ultimately must fit.

This tendency was at a maximum in an era of constitutional interpretation that suggested that the meaning of the Constitution and therefore of the First Amendment was fixed by its historical context. This, in turn, meant that the state of liberty in the country was vitally affected by historical evidence on original intentions. Under these conditions, it was hard to approach reconstruction of history "as it really was" with any great objectivity.

To some extent, our current attitude toward judicial interpretation alters this situation. "Judicial fundamentalism" still plays a role in constitutional interpretation; indeed, as we have seen, Black has quite cogently welded together such an approach with far-reaching doctrines for political change. Yet the moving spirit of the times and the specific intent of the author of a provision are regarded as something of a will-o'-the-wisp, a snipe chase that gets you nothing at its most successful and keeps you running purposelessly at its worst. As Hughes observed crisply in the Minnesota Moratorium Case,

> If by the statement that what the Constitution meant at the time of its adoption is what it means today, it is intended to say that the great clauses of the Constitution must be confined to the interpretation, which the framers, with the conditions and outlook of their time would have placed upon them, the statement carries its own refutation.[1]

In the Segregation Case, the Court despaired even more of ascertaining historical meanings: "[W]e cannot turn the clock

---

1. *Home Building and Loan Association* v. *Blaisdell*, 290 U.S. 398 (1934), pp. 442–3.

back to 1868 when the Amendment was adopted, or even to 1896 when *Plessy v. Ferguson* was written."[2] Implicit, too, in this statement is the basic attitude that the peculiar intent of constitutional framers is relevant information in arriving at a contemporary meaning for a legal provision, but it is not determinative even if ascertainable. In consequence of this contemporary attitude, rationalized in various forms, scholars may now stare at constitutional history with more attention to the actual setting of a controversial provision and less consciousness of helping determine their own fates as citizens. This hardly eliminates all problems of objectivity, but it does permit a constitutional history less immediately result-oriented. "Lawyers' history"—designed to buttress a case—can be left to the lawyers.

Nonetheless, it is still inevitable that writing on the history of freedom often reflects the dominant interests, concerns, and themes of its time. Freedom, indeed, is all too often one of those central concerns. With what John Roche has referred to as the need for "retrospective symmetry," the Founders are imputed significant attitudes on contemporary concerns or are interpreted in the light of contemporary ideology.

ERAS OF CONSTITUTIONAL INTERPRETATION

In general, historical interpretations of the First Amendment can be subsumed under three headings. The dominant opinion during the early years was highly conservative, in an almost literal sense, emphasizing the notion that the Constitution was intended to secure (or safeguard) rights already available to Englishmen. All but a few significant writers on the First Amendment saw it largely in Blackstonian terms as aimed at preventing censorship, that is, as guaranteeing free-

---

2. *Brown* v. *Board of Education,* 347 U.S. 483 (1954), p. 492.

dom (or lack of prior restraint) of the press. Subsequent punishment was not, however, viewed, as violating the constitutional requirement in this view, which tended to dominate nineteenth-century writing. Blackstone's definition was cited with monotonous regularity, and it seems worthwhile to repeat the litany here:

> The liberty of the press is indeed essential to the nature of a free state; but this consists in laying no *previous* restraints upon publication, and not in freedom from censure for criminal matter when published. Every freeman has an undoubted right to lay what sentiments he pleases before the public: to forbid this is to destroy the freedom of the press; but if he publishes what is improper, mischievous, or illegal, he must take the consequences of his own temerity.[3]

No standards for subsequent punishment were developed by Blackstone, so that only the most fearless were protected in their expression.

The first quarter of the twentieth century saw consolidation of the position earlier advanced only by stray, although highly significant and influential writers and occasional political movements. The First Amendment was viewed as decidedly more significant, controlling and limiting subsequent punishment and primarily aimed at out-lawing seditious libel—that is, trying individuals on criminal charges for criticism of government or its officials. In more recent years, the intent of the clause was seen as aimed at very broad interdiction of governmental power, both prior and subsequent to publication.

Finally, within the past decade or so, a revisionist mood has prevailed—particularly under the influence of Leonard Levy's important book, *Legacy of Suppression.*[4] In this view —virtually a Federalist one—the First Amendment is indeed

---

3. Blackstone, *Commentaries on the Law of England* (Thomas Cooley, ed.; Chicago: Callagha Co. 1884), Bk. IV, sec. 152.
4. Leonard Levy, *Legacy of Suppression* (Cambridge, Mass.: Harvard University Press, 1960).

merely a reaffirmation of English Common Law provisions and therefore of little protective value, until the early years of the nineteenth century; then, as a consequence of the Alien and Sedition Federalist efforts at suppression and reciprocal failures of the Democratic-Republicans to use state machinery for prosecution of their opponents for seditious libel, a tradition of freedom emerged. The legacy of suppression was a mixture of grudging tolerance and principled empathy resulting from the mutuality of partisan experience, and this attitude has prevailed. It is interesting that in the important New York Times *v.* Sullivan Case, which finally —some eight score years after this historical consensus developed—gave legal impetus to the end of seditious libel, Levy's history was cited with apparent acceptance. Such a view created no apparent worries for the Justices about the binding nature of the original meanings attached to the First Amendment.

The quick and dirty outline sketched in the previous paragraphs requires obvious qualification and considerable elaboration. The proposition that the freedom of press guaranteed by the Constitution is identical with a no-licensing provision has historically been rejected by writers of prominence in every era, particularly those in the Jeffersonian tradition. The controversy over the passage and implementation of the Alien and Sedition Acts explicitly challenged that notion—limiting the Amendment to approving the common law as it stood in 1789—and engendered a political consensus that was reflected in legal writings, although not in legal decisions at the federal level. The Jeffersonian states'-rights argument was actually as uncompromising as that of Justice Black: the Federal Government has no role in the field of free speech. Although sedition as a concept was also attacked —most particularly criticized was the notion of a common law federal crime of sedition—the thrust of Jeffersonianism was to give a monopoly on repression of opinion to the states. Therefore, the corrective to the Alien and Sedition Acts was seen as sufficiently established by failure to re-enact such legislation and by financial recompense to victims as provided for by congressional enactment. All of this was accomplished outside of the court structure, so that only the issue of whether there were common law crimes under federal law remained to be adjudicated, and this resulted in a further Jeffersonian triumph in the United States *v.* Hudson and Goodwin.

However, commentators on the Constitution were not lacking, and they often denied Blackstone's major premises, although perhaps on slender legal grounds. As early as 1803, St. George Tucker, in his American edition of Blackstone, suggested that Blackstone's views deal only with England, "which is very different from the footing upon which it stands in the United States," where constitutionally there is guaranteed "absolute and uncontrollable right of speaking, writing and publishing our opinions concerning any subject." This Jeffersonian legal theorist expressed himself most emphatically that "the federal government is destitute of all such authority."[5] Following Madison's own reply to the justification of the Alien and Sedition laws offered by a House committee in 1799, the anti-Federalists, including Tucker and George Hay, espoused doctrines that clearly transcended Blackstone, however much they might have lacked to a modern eye. Even more directly, Thomas Cooley, a most influential writer and state judge, found that more was logically immanent in the Amendment, else:

> . . . The liberty of the press might be rendered a mockery. . . . The evils to be prevented were not the censorship

---

5. St. George Tucker, Appendix G, Vol. I, Pt. II, *Blacktone's Commentaries* (Philadelphia: William Young Birch & Abraham Small, 1803), pp. 11, 18, 24. The discussion on pp. 11–30 is written in impassioned terms, repeatedly asserting "absolute" freedom of expression, and is relied on heavily by Black in his concurrence in the New York Times Case. An accessible extract of this and other historically significant statements can be found in Levy's excellent compilation, *Freedom of the Press from Zenger to Jefferson* (Indianapolis: The Bobbs-Merrill Company, Inc., 1966).

of the press merely, but any action of the government by means of which it might prevent such free and general discussion of public matters as seems absolutely essential to prepare the people for an intelligent exercise of their rights as citizens.[6]

During and after World War I, liberal writers also met the sedition prosecutions of that era by systematically seeking constitutional limits to governmental authority. On the federal level, the leading figure in this scholarly venture, Zechariah Chafee, Jr., was personally and ideologically identified with the most prominent judicial spokesman for such limitations, Oliver Wendell Holmes. As Harry Kalven has pointed out in his quest to make Holmes the major figure in the continual development of liberty, Chafee tended both to minimize the role of others—even Brandeis—and to move from the central focus of legal analysis matters not dealt with by Holmes. Historically, Chafee suggested the First Amendment more or less resolved the major problems, leaving Holmes to provide the final clue, the clear and present danger formula. (Actually, Chafee interpreted the latter as involving more of an "overt act" test—that is, government should step in to prevent actions not to punish words—then Holmes, at least on the surface, emphasized, but Chafee purported to follow Holmes.) Of early history, Chafee's discussion is tentative and fragmentary, but occasionally his conclusions burst forth in absolute and unsupported terms. Thus, Chafee affirmed that the First Amendment intended "to wipe out the common law of sedition and make further prosecutions for criticism of the government without any incitement to law-breaking forever impossible in the United States of America."[7] Much the same can be said of Henry Schofield's ex-

---

6. Thomas Cooley, *Constitutional Limitations* (8th ed.; Boston: Little, Brown & Co., 1927), 885.

7. Zechariah Chafee, Jr., *Free Speech in the United States* (Cambridge, Mass: Harvard University Press, 1941), p. 21.

tremely important, and somewhat earlier, essay on "Freedom of the Press in the United States." Schofield argued that "the constitutional declarations of liberty of the press are original works of the American people in the sphere of law and government," and that "one of the objects of the Revolution was to get rid of the English common law on liberty of speech and press."[8] On the whole it is fair to say, as Leonard Levy has, that these conclusions became articles of a liberal orthodoxy that tended to dwell on the stray bits of strong conclusions and to ignore the fragilities of data (and even contradictory evidence) on which these conclusions purportedly rested.

In reaction, Levy has struck back with rather strong conclusions of his own, asserting that:

> [T]he First Amendment was not intended to supersede the common law of seditious libel, that the legislatures rather than the courts were the chief suppressing agencies, that the theory of freedom of speech in political matters was quite narrow until 1798, that English libertarian theory was in the vanguard of the American, that the Bill of Rights was in large measure a lucky political accident and that the First Amendment was more an expression of federalism than of libertarianism.[9]

Donald Meiklejohn has quite correctly suggested that "the contrast between Chafee's history and Levy's history is in fact not very sharp." Chafee acknowledged in his book that the Framers "say very little about its exact meaning," which did not emerge clearly until the sedition law "made the limits of the liberty of the press a concrete and burning issue."[10] Wallace Mendelson (as well as Levy, who explicitly relies on Mendelson), quotes very similar statements by

---

8. Henry Schofield, "Freedom of the Press in the United States," *Papers and Proceedings of the American Sociological Society* (1915), 114, 76.
9. Leonard Levy, Preface to *Freedom of Speech and Press in Early American History* (paper ed., originally titled *Legacy of Suppression;* New York: Harper & Row, 1963), p. ix.
10. Donald Meiklejohn, *Southern California Law Review,* XXXV, No. 3 (1961), 112, 113, and quoting Chafee, *Free Speech,* p. 16.

Chafee and suggests that, in his later years, he had a change of heart. But the quoted sentiment and many other passages like it appear in Chafee's 1920 book as well as in later efforts.[11] Perhaps even more striking is the Wechsler formulation of the dispute, a formula lifted bodily from his brief in the New York Times Case and incorporated into the majority opinion by Mr. Justice Brennan:

> This is the lesson to be drawn from the great controversy over the Sedition Act of 1798, 1 Stat. b 596, *which first crystallized a national awareness of the central meaning of the First Amendment.* See Levy, *Legacy of Suppression* (1960), at 258 et seq [emphasis added].[12]

As Kalven points out, this formula neatly avoids the problem of historical meaning and, at the same time, obviously incorporates Levy's revisionism. But one cannot help wondering as to whether it was consciously or unconsciously that Wechsler chose to echo Chafee's parallel observation that "the meaning of the First Amendment did not crystallize in 1791."[13] Levy, in focusing on the extreme statements of the libertarians, attacks neither straw men nor caricatures, since their own statements have led to misapprehensions, but he does less than justice to his subjects. (Thus Holmes is criticized for asserting that, "I wholly disagree with the argument that the First Amendment left the common law as to seditious libel in force. History seems to me against the notion." Yet the continuation of that statement is, "I had conceived that the United States through many years had shown its

---

11. See Chafee, *Freedom of Speech* (New York: Harcourt, Brace & World, Inc., 1920), pp. 17, 32, for the identical language quoted above. Compare Mendelson "On the Meaning of the First Amendment: Absolutes in the Balance," *California Law Review,* XXX (1962), 823, and Levy *Freedom of Speech and Press in Early American History,* p. xix, for claims Chaffee was recanting.
12. *New York Times* v. *Sullivan,* 376 U.S. 254 (1964), p. 273.
13. Chafee, *Freedom of Speech,* p. 32. His statement, there, might well be Levy's "Liberty of Speech is no more confined to the speech they thought permissible than commerce . . . to the vehicles of 1780."

repentence for the Sedition Act . . . by repaying fines that it imposed,"[14] a statement that suggests Holmes' understanding of history was one virtually indistinguishable from Levy's.) Schofield and Chafee had emphasized a desire for change, but suggested that the scope of change was not readily understood. Levy chooses to emphasize the absence of a well-defined and consistent libertarian thought and attributes a specific and narrow meaning to the First Amendment, while suggesting that later developments were made possible by chance use of broad language—the latter representing the framers' gift for "studied imprecision."[15]

Thus, even with qualifications, then, the same general picture emerges today. The historiography of the First Amendment itself demands historical elaboration of no small moment. The extremes of interpretation have not been tamed and the variety of interpretations continue to be rather notable.

To a large extent, this disagreement represents recurrent, almost universal differences of temperament and attitude toward government and power. It re-enacts the traditional Hamiltonian–Jeffersonian drama of American differences. Some writers attempt to solve the problem by regarding the Founding Fathers as coherently agreeing in a philosophy fundamentally Federalist in nature. Thus, Justice Harlan has observed that the Founding Fathers "staked their faith that liberty would prosper in the new nation not primarily upon declarations of individual rights but upon the kind of government the union was to have."[16] Again, Willmoore Kendall has built an elaborate edifice in favor of less libertarianism by reading the phrases of the Preamble as limitations on the First Amendment, that is, freedom of expression is allowed as long as it contributes to the general

---

14. *Abrams* v. *United States,* 250 U.S. 616, 630 (1919).
15. The phrase is that of Meiklejohn, book review, *Southern California Law Review,* XXXV 117.
16. John Harlan, "The Bill of Rights and the Constitution: An Excerpt From an Address," *Columbia Law Review,* LXIV (1964), 1175, 1176.

welfare, and so forth, but may be suppressed if it detracts from domestic tranquillity and the other general goals of the Preamble.[17] Such an interpretation might have some persuasiveness—though it would hardly be compelling—if the Constitution had been a monolith in its construction and legal enaction. But, as the late Alexander Pekelis brilliantly pointed out, the Bill of Rights is the last compromise of the Constitution—an external one. Further, he noted that the fundamental gulf between the points of view of the advocates of these two portions of the document are well suggested by the opening operative words; in the first instance, they are positive assertions of power: "All legislative power herein granted shall be vested in a Congress;" in the second, the anti-Federalists suggest their almost anarchic fear of power: "Congress shall make no law."[18]

This fundamental difference in point of view toward power and government has persisted throughout our history; it has sometimes been mitigated, but it also has at times been exacerbated by the fact that many Americans respond to both appeals.[19]

THE HISTORY OF THE FIRST AMENDMENT

History is always delphic; but the origins of the First Amendment are even sphinxlike. The Amendment was virtually not discussed in the Congress, not even those aspects that were novel. Its author, Madison, left few clues, and, of

---

17. Willmore Kendall, "Baloney *v.* Free Speech, *National Review* (May 22, 1962), 367–8.
18. Alexander Pekelis, *Law and Social Action* (Ithaca, N.Y.: Cornell University Press, 1950), p. 94.
19. Levy suggests adoption was no necessity and was intended to have little consequence. But even Fisher Ames, whose mocking of the Bill of Rights is second in belittlement only to Bentham's and whose federalist credentials are impeccable, felt political pressures required the move. "It is necessary to conciliate and I would have amendments" (Letter to Minot, July 23, 1789, *Works of Fisher Ames* [Boston: Little, Brown and Co., 1854], p. 65).

these, his latter-day comments could not fail to be politically tainted.

There is one thing we can positively say, and that is negative in nature. Mr. Justice Black has suggested that it is no accident that the First Amendment is first in ordering, and Edmond Cahn has made a similar point. In fact, however, no such import can be read into the ordering. To begin with, Madison sought to amend the Constitution through internal emendations and additions rather than through an external appendix. Indeed, by far the bulk of the contemporary debate extant on the entire Bill of Rights concerns itself with this question of form rather than the substance or sequence of the proposals. At no point, in either the listed demands of the several states or in Madison's list—indeed not even in the group of amendments proposed by the House and sent to the Senate or even those offered for ratification to the states—did the First Amendment head all of the rest. It was the rejection of priority amendments on apportionment of representatives and compensation—surely historical accident—that resulted in the positioning of those of Madison's proposals adopted.

If we turn from the course of events to the actual debates, the meager discussions seem to provide little guidance. On the whole, they seem to bear out Levy's statement that no one expressed even a veiled desire to eliminate seditious libel. Some writers see, through highly interpretative reading, a precise constitutional argument in Madison's statements, but to a more casual eye these comments approach the level of pieties. At least one side comment appears worthy of note, in that it indicates that the state of American liberties was so strong and the presumptions for a right to criticize political office holders so powerful that Congress would not even punish scurrilous remarks about itself.[20]

---

20. See the statement of Mr. Jackson, June 8, 1789. The full text of the debates are conveniently available in Bennett B. Patterson, *The Forgotten Ninth Amendment* (Indianapolis: the Bobbs-Merrill Company,

Investigation of antecedents of the First Amendment uncovers no burning zeal for broad new guarantees. The post-revolutionary period did indeed witness enactment of a number of state constitutional provisions, but they were often explicitly conservative in the protection afforded. Similarly, the official, usually convention minority, requests for amendments, which the ratifying state conventions forwarded with approval following the strategy set by Massachusetts, neither gave prominence to libertarian impulses, nor contained novelties in wording and specificity. To be sure, the general rhetoric was libertarian but at such a plane of generality as to be irrelevant to our concerns.

Faced with so conservative an historical record, one is tempted to assert with the judges of the nineteenth century that the Amendment was intended merely to incorporate the Blackstonian approach—the mere prohibition of censorship. Unfortunately for simplicity's sake, this meaning of the Amendment seems unlikely, and the notion that it is merely declaratory of the existing common-law standards is unconvincing on the evidence of the text itself.

Of these indications, the strongest and most perplexing is the inclusion of protection for freedom of speech. It is clear that protection of freedom of speech cannot involve merely "no prior censorship," which, of course, has little meaning at all with regard to regulation of speech. The casual inclusion of this wording when coupled with rejection of such constraint on the states suggests a desire to protect something deemed a genuine right.

This provision was itself novel; the traditional context of the phrase "freedom of speech" had been in connection with the right of the parliamentary Speaker, who was granted immunity to convey that body's requests without punishment

---

Inc., 1955); see p. 119. In the light of Levy's statements on legislative intolerance, Jackson's assurance that no persecutions were conceivable, that "these are principles which will always prevail," indicates a change in public attitude.

from the king; indeed, that was the origin of his title. Then the right of expression was extended to protect all legislators from accountability for comments during official proceedings. This traditional privilege had already been incorporated into the Constitution in Article I, Section 4.

From the provisions of various state constitutions and early charters, a pattern may be gleaned suggesting a further evolution more tenuous than Meiklejohn's notions but in accordance with them. That is to say, there is some evidence of an expanding scope of those held to be entitled to freedom of speech—from the Speaker, to members of a legislature, to those chosen to participate in representative town meetings, to those involved in town meetings, and later to the electorate.[21]

Generally, the choice of language historically involved—describing the rights of those engaged in the people's business—seems peculiarly appropriate. When giving authority to the mass of people to comment on their own business, this invocation of words with a political history looms as an interesting support for the Meiklejohn thesis. By the same token, it creates problems for Levy's interpretation, problems not wholly met in his book. He argues, quite reasonably in connection with the meaning of "freedom of the press," that one cannot lightly impute an intent to use a legal doctrine in a sense other than its historical one without some evidence of a change of heart. Yet, it is apparent that the Congress adopted a new usage of "freedom of speech" in the same breath without a murmur on the part of a single member. To that date, only the Pennsylvania Constitution of 1776 mentioned freedom of speech. Levy suggests that this bears out his position: "History . . . shows that . . . the only one of the original states to protect constitutionally both speech and press did not intend to abandon the common law of seditious libel."[22] But, in fact, even the Pennsylvania provision does

---

21. See Mary P. Clarke, *Parliamentary Privilege in the American Colonies* (New Haven, Conn.: Yale University Press, 1943), esp. pp. 62 *ff.*
22. Levy, *Freedom of Speech and Press . . .* , p. 185.

not protect free speech; in something of a non-sequitur, it merely buttresses freedom of the press by a reference to the need for freedom of speech.[23] Only in 1790 did the right of speech become an independent one even in Pennsylvania. In form therefore, as a separate and distinctive right, the First Amendment represents an even greater departure than Levy suggests.

Indeed, by the simple process of focusing on different clauses of the Amendment, writers can suggest different modes of interpretation as appropriate. By focusing on freedom of the press—appropriately enough for a discussion of the law of seditious libel—Levy argues for a narrow view of the Amendment. By focusing on freedom of speech, others call attention to the innovating function of the Amendment. By emphasizing the religious establishment clause, the motive force can be viewed as states' rights.

In another important respect, there seems to be evidence against the Bill of Rights merely being an exercise in the statement of the obvious. The wording of the Amendment also belies casualness, since, for all the lack of discussion, it appears that several changes of phraseology took place in the course of adoption. At virtually every stage—excepting only the conference level—such alterations did occur.

Perhaps the most inconvenient aspect of the matter is the overwhelming evidence that, in at least one important matter, the prevailing attitude was unmistakably a deviation from the then current attitude in British common law and that that deviation also was not the subject of extensive debate. The English law of libel could properly be said to have been in ferment, although, in the eyes of authoritative judges, the common law was clear; the corrective in England came about through legislation rather than interpretation. The question disputed was the celebrated one of the Zenger Case—whether the jury in a libel case has only the function

---

23. ". . . *The people* have a right to freedom of speech, and of writing, and
     publishing their sentiments; therefore the freedom of the press ought
     not to be restrained" (Pennsylvania, *Constitution* [1776], Art. XII.

of passing on the fact of publication or can move into the domain of whether the statements involved constituted a libel and the motive or intent to commit a libel. This question of authority was substantively important, for jurors, when allowed to rule on the question of what was a libel, had historically insisted on letting off defendants who proved their statements, whereas the judges and the precedents clung to the absurdity of "the greater the truth the greater the libel." Fox's Libel Act (1792) gave the functional victory to those advocating a change in Great Britain, and subsequent legislation also established truth as a defense.[24]

Both of these bits of remedial action postdated the Amendment, and any tough-minded assumption that the First Amendment was shorthand for the state of British Common Law of 1789 would suggest that on the federal level, the United States law would not have incorporated these changes. Yet even the much despised Alien and Sedition Acts provided for truth as a defense, accepted Erskine's test that there had to be an *intent* to commit sedition, and vindicated the right of the jury to rule on the truth of the matter. Thus, as Harry Kalven points out, on paper the Alien and Sedition Acts were more liberal than Fox's Libel Act—the latter a much praised move. To be sure, the judges emasculated the truth and intent provisions of the Sedition Act by such requirements as that a single witness be introduced to prove truth of the whole of any matter in dispute, a crippling requirement in all but the most trivial and simple of allegations.[25]

In an interesting brief overview of Anglo-Saxon traditions on freedom of speech and freedom of press, A. L. Goodhart suggests a middle way: the First Amendment was remedial precisely as in Fox's Libel Act, and the constitu-

---

24. The form of Fox's libel law suggests the Act was merely a reaffirmation of existing law, but the debates show a consciousness that reform was taking place. See Morris Forkosch, "Freedom of the Press: Crosswell's Case," *Fordham Law Review,* XXXIII (1965), 415, 427.
25. See Harry Kalven, *The Negro and the First Amendment* (Columbus: Ohio State University Press, 1965), p. 20.

tional affront was in the rulings of the judges who clung to the backward precedents of earlier years.[26] But (1) Levy found no evidence of a push for even such a change; (2) the argument of unconstitutionality was leveled even 'against the Act itself, which was, as we have noted, "ameliorative" of the common law. So the matter remains murky no matter how we turn. One resolution is to suggest the Framers accepted the argument stressed by them in the prerevolutionary era, that the position, say, of Andrew Hamilton in the Zenger Case was the correct interpretation of the common law. One difficulty is that the anti-federalists had expressly suggested the Constitution threatened trial of such matters without juries.[27]

The hostile reception of the Acts, clearly more libertarian than the existing British legislation of the day in 1798, and therefore *a fortiori* more libertarian than the state of the common law at the time of the Amendment's enactment, has its own constitutional force and was predicated on constitutional grounds. Levy himself concedes that a libertarian tide, a "climate of opinion for liberty," was developing before the enactment of the bills but argues that during that period libertarian arguments still were party justifications for self-expression for themselves, lacking mature realization that their logic also required rights for others. It would appear safe to follow Chafee and Holmes here in suggesting that at least a substantial portion of the population raised a question of constitutionality quickly, unequivocally, and without a sense on their part of sham—all within a generation of adoption of the Bill of Rights.

Levy's conclusion is that there was "no passion on the part of anyone to grind underfoot the common law. . . ."[28] Part of this is due to his rather strict standard for accepting as established advocacy of a change—absolute consistency in the exposition of ideas on freedom or a very precise statement

---

26. A. L. Goodhart, "Freedom of Speech and Freedom of Press," *Washington University Law Quarterly* (1964), 257–9.
27. See, for example, Jackson Turner Main, *The Anti-Federalists* (Chapel Hill: University of Carolina Press, 1961), pp. 160–1.
28. Levy, *Freedom of Speech and Press . . .* , p. 233.

in legal terms of some definite modification of the common law. It would appear that, given this standard, his conclusions are basically sound. But this standard is somewhat peculiar, if not misleading. Levy suggests that the generalized rhetoric of freedom of expression must be disregarded, that it was a cloak for the more standard position that truth (which every advocate regarded as equivalent to his own position) was to be allowed. Under the guise of universalistic arguments, the framers were in fact making self-serving claims.

At least two qualifications seem in order. The generation of Americans who framed the First Amendment had engaged in considerable thought and had come a long way with respect to toleration of religious differences and were quite familiar with notions of diverse approaches to religious truth. Many of the free-speech doctrines Levy does not find in eighteenth-century America were clearly urged with respect to religion.[29] Secondly, even if Levy were proved correct with regard to the human obtuseness and self-interest of the framers, the influence of utilization and repetition of generalized arguments for freedom—particularly in the light of the state of the discussion on religion—must have had its impact. The seeds of the future were already there before the Federalist fiasco of the Alien and Sedition Acts.

THE EVIDENCE OF POSTAMENDMENT HISTORY

A more comprehensive, precise statement than Levy's perhaps emerges from the writings of Ernst Freund in 1917 (a statement that represents his reading of Schofield, generally considered the fount of the libertarian position).

In the course of the eighteenth century, however, a further struggle took place, for greater freedom. . . . Our bills of

---

29. See Samuel Krislov, "Mr. Justice Black Reopens the Free Speech Debate," *UCLA Law Review,* XI (1964), 189, 204n, for some examples.

rights reflect this stage of development; they guarantee impunity for true matter published, but only if published with good motives. Here most of our constitutional guarantees stop; but the practice of the nineteenth century has proceeded far beyond this.[30]

It would appear appropriate to dichotomize the traditions of freedom: to suggest that popular attitudes on constitutional liberties had very early far outstripped constitutional decisions, which were in fact rendered largely unnecessary, partly by the public attitude, particularly toward national action, and partly by the changes in legal attitude signaled by the private-law developments called to our attention by Freund. As Sir James Fitzjames Stephen points out, such a change is implicit in the alteration of the basic relationship of rulers and populace that took place in the late eighteenth and early nineteenth centuries:

> Two different views may be taken of the relation between rulers and their subjects. If the ruler is regarded as the superior of the subject, as being by the nature of his position presumably wise and good, the rightful ruler and guide of the whole population, it must necessarily follow that it is wrong to censure him openly; that even if he is mistaken his mistakes should be pointed out with the utmost respect, and that whether mistaken or not no censure should be cast upon him likely or designed to diminish his authority.
>
> If on the other hand the ruler is regarded as the agent and servant, and the subject as the wise and good master who is obliged to delegate his power to the so-called ruler because being a multitude he cannot use it himself, it is obvious that this sentiment must be reversed. Every member of the public who censures the ruler for the time being exercises in his own person the right which belongs to the whole of which he forms a part. He is finding fault with his servant.[31]

---

30. Freund, p. 15.
31. James Fitzjames Stephen, *History of the Criminal Law of England,* II (London: Macmillan and Co., 1883), 299.

As this change in attitude took place—somewhat earlier in the United States than in England—the judges began to deal with discussions of public officials as "privilege" or "fair comment," comparing it to the right of employers to evaluate services rendered or critics to comment on a play or work of art. Whereas the public talked in broad constitutional terms, the judges found protection of freedom of speech in very narrow common-law analogies.

With short-term exceptions mainly about the time of the Civil War, the fundamental power has been with the states, and, largely, the issue has been one of their practice—a highly checkerboarded matter. Not until the twentieth century were such state issues to become national constitutional ones, with the emphasis on Supreme Court intervention at the state level. This, in turn, generated pressures that have been felt in constitutional law at the federal level by a process Glendon Schubert has described as "reverse incorporation." That is to say, attention to matters of self-expression first attracted Supreme Court concern at the state level, and this then attracted concern at the national level.

This outline is at variance with that of those who postulate a golden era of a perfect yeoman-farmer society, in which impediments to freedom—legal, economic, or social—were virtually nonexistent. Such a position, to be sure, is a caricature of that taken by any of the major writers discussed, but it is, as we have noted, unfortunately a caricature for which some of these same figures have agreed to sit.

The attitude that legal progress in the defense of freedom has been made in the past two centuries, rather than a condition of degeneracy having set in, hardly seems discouraging or unrealistic. Living in a much more centralized society with its greater potential threats to individualism, the twentieth-century American has inevitably sought legal re-enforcement for rights formerly cloaked in personal anonymity and protected by the weakness of bureaucratic techniques. Looking back over history, at the height of the

McCarthyism controversy, John P. Roche, a colleague both institutionally and intellectually of Levy, suggested in a series of articles that "we never had more freedom." This theme— developed in more systematic fashion in his "American Liberty: An Examination of the Tradition of Freedom,"[32]— emphasizes change and elaboration in legal protection to keep pace with social complexity. Formerly he saw little legal protection for expression of dissent; rather, he saw a social structure loosely hung together with many enclaved groups, permitting one to move within a friendly ambiance of limited nature. Freedom inhered in the isolation of social classes from one another, in the insulation of diverse groups from at least some of the ramifications of wider social control. Within these groupings, little atmosphere of wide-scale tolerance prevailed. Americans could affiliate with the conformism of their choice, and diversity existed in this insular fashion, seldom coming into the ken of a relatively intolerant, but inefficient legal order.

What seems to have made the system work in the nine-teenth century was the more-or-less coincidence of important groupings within state or, more accurately, regional lines. Thus, the national government, after a few abortive efforts at damping abolitionist zeal, left the problem to the localities, permitting increasing deviation in the states, which ranged from outright repression to semisovereign support. The emergence of national standards for liberty can be explicitly viewed as a by-product of nationalization of values and the emergence of an American community.

Here lies the difference between the "golden dream" advocates, who would see this as merely a conscious recognition of an inheritance always ours, and the evolutionists, who suggest that an historical development has occurred in consonance with that inheritance. Evolutionists, thus, necessarily

---

32. John P. Roche, "American Liberty: An Examination of the Tradition of Freedom in Milton Konvitz and Clinton Rossiter, *Aspects of Liberty* (Ithaca: Cornell University Press, 1958), pp. 129–62.

sacrifice some legitimation gained by antiquity and must accept some notion of change as possible, indeed probable, in the future.

Some of this loss can be cut, for it is plausible to argue—as does Charles Curtis, for example—that the justification of permissible change within the American tradition is both a meaningful concept and an operating constraint; in this sense, the future constitutional law is reflected in and limited by both the present and past. It may seem to be of little consequence whether one roots a free-press position in the spirit of the First Congress or in the first political and presidential transition. Nonetheless, one is obviously more subject to possible revisionism in the light of history—particularly since the attitude of a determinate body can be discussed no matter how vaguely—whereas appeal to an indefinite and vaguely defined tradition can always be stated to permit greater legitimized deviations in further conduct. It is, however, doubtful that any social myth of the Founding Fathers determining our political freedom is either necessary or sufficient to ensure public support, particularly if, in fact, this notion appears historically incorrect or inadequate.

PROPERTY RIGHTS AND PERSONAL RIGHTS

A closely related question about the "tradition of liberty" results from the dichotomization of property rights and personal rights. We have already discussed the preferred-freedoms approach, which suggests that the saliency of political freedom is a value to be defended. With Roche's "retrospective symmetry," advocates have postulated a consistent predisposition throughout our history toward that attitude. Conversely, others—suggestively enough, usually less libertarian or activist—write American history in terms of a tradition of defense of property, used largely in the Lockean and pre-Lockean sense of those things pertaining to self and self-realization, but also in the more recent sense of physical ownership.

The notion of basic inalienable human rights is itself Lockean and finds its expression in early Court decisions, most conspicuously as in Washington's rambling, vague, and largely irrelevant discussions in Corfield *v.* Coryell. It also is as contemporary as last week's Court decision. The question as to what has been the basic mode of American thought is again largely based on one's orientation to the future, rather than a determination of particulars. If one turns to the historical record, the indications are that libertarians have blown out of proportion the emphasis on "what are now called civil liberties."[33]

An even more accurate statement would be that the distinction between human rights and property rights is in fact one of recent connection. It is also one that can be explained in terms of the decline of the importance of "real," "personal" property, as opposed to securities and other forms of intangible property. There was always recognition of the fact that attributes of ownership were a means to an end, and that end the traditional liberal program said to be "maximization of the human will." But the same limitation exists as to the utility of each constitutional liberty, for each is essentially instrumental, too. Thus, if we turn to historical discussions we will then find little guidance as to any particular hierarchy of freedoms, for the comprehensiveness of the language does not allow us to determine which of the liberties is truly being pressed.

If we turn to the judiciary, we may note that the usual bias in the common law is particularly toward cases based on damages, that is, involving a complaint of deprivation with compensation on analogy to the basic form of action, trespass.

---

33. The phrase is quoted from a reply by the late Learned Hand to an inquiry of mine on February 19, 1954. I have always considered it an indication of the pace of civil liberties adjudication in the 1930s and 1940s.

Regardless of the constitutional meaning of the First Amendment, it was therefore inevitable that the judicial meaning would be essentially one involving property rights. The great cases that defined liberty of expression involved defamation, the right to a calling, and freedom to utilize and acquire skills. The history of litigation on civil liberties has indeed been largely one in which the issue has been presented in property terms.

Charles Warren, one of the proponents of the "property matrix" notion, called attention to this fact in the 1920s, arguing, in essence, that the new emphasis on human rights was a corruption of the constitutional system. In his *Liberty Against Government,* Edward Corwin treats the same history in identical terms as a natural, evolutionary development with which he shows occasional personal irritation.[34] Yet, in the face of such contrary eminent authority—and conceding the practical import of their histories—it is possible to suggest that even the judiciary did not so much deprecate purely human rights as regard them as outside the scope of government, of authority, and even court concern. The principal vehicle for protection of First Amendment rights is, concededly, the political process, and it was a combination of self-corrective action in the political sphere with judiciary inactivity that severely limited the effectiveness of the courts.

Above all, the federal limitation meant that the domain of the United States courts was severely limited with respect to those aspects of free expression that operatively affected their day-to-day exercise in the theatre that counted, the domain of state and local governments. In a sense, a well-developed corpus of Supreme Court law would have largely been an exercise in futility as long as the states were free to create restrictions without review.

---

34. Charles Warren, "The New 'Liberty' Under the Fourteenth Amendment," *Harvard Law Review,* XXXIX (1926), 431; Edward Corwin, *Liberty Against Government* (Baton Rouge: Louisiana State University Press, 1948).

THE CENTRAL IMPORTANCE OF THE FOURTEENTH AMENDMENT

All of this was changed by the Fourteenth Amendment. The ramifications of the provision have been extensive and far-reaching, best summarized in two trends. One, well-known and well-analyzed, has been the process of reading in, as implicit in the Fourteenth Amendment, application to the states of various legal standards of the Bill of Rights applying to the national government. The effect of this incorporation process has been to apply the same standards to both national and state governments and to transfer authority over enforcement to the federal courts. This process, which the late Justice Frankfurter derided as equating the word "liberty" in the Fourteenth Amendment with a shorthand symbol for the Bill of Rights, has been instrumental in nationalizing basic freedoms, extending them in scope throughout our country, and in revitalizing their interpretation.

The second tendency has been somewhat less clearcut and manifest. The application of federal standards to state regulations on liberty has been paralleled by adoption of more stringent requirements on the national level. Focusing on state standards has resulted in calling attention to restrictions implicit in the federal standards. This process, as we have noted, Glendon Schubert has identified—with tongue tight against cheek—as "reverse incorporation." It is hardly a clearcut case of cause and effect; changes in society and law and the emergence of new groups like the ACLU all contributed to this development.[35]

The process of incorporation was indeed a long one and one which has interested—and, no doubt, over-interested—constitutional historians. The ink was hardly dry on the ratification of the Fourteenth Amendment, with its seeming guarantees of national rights of citizenship, before efforts

---

35. See Samuel Krislov, "The Amicus Curiae Brief: From Friendship to Advocacy," *Yale Law Journal*, LXXII (1963), 694.

were made to have the Court oversee all state legislation affecting property rights by using the privileges and immunity clause of the Fourteenth Amendment—efforts that were rebuffed in the Slaughter House Cases. A decade of further effort resulted in quite a different result, for, in the Minnesota Rate Cases, the Court found it a denial of liberty without due process of law if a state established a rate of property for a public carrier while precluding judicial review of the propriety of that rate. As the distinguished judge and teacher Charles Hough observed, "It is from that decision that I date the flood."[36] For four decades thereafter, economic legislation by state governments was thoroughly censored by the courts on the theory that the Fourteenth Amendment required meeting national standards of justice before property could be compromised. Human rights, however, were not judicially protected, the legal analogue of railroader Robert Young's effective slogan of the 1940s, "a hog can cross the country without changing trains, but you can't." This anomaly could not easily be defended.

As early as Hurtado *v.* California,[37] the Court discovered rights "fundamental" that might define due process of law, and this distinction was to be used sometimes without noting the source. The Court distinguished sharply, for the first time deciding the case on this basis, between fundamental rights, identified as historically and logically indispensable, and mere convenience or arrangements designed to implement or buttress basic rights. The former were, the Court acknowledged, protected by the Fourteenth Amendment, but this was by virtue of the imperatives of its own phraseology rather than because of specific provisions of the remainder of the Constitution. The latter, the subsidiary rights, were not protected at all by the federal Constitution.

---

36. Charles Hough, "Due Process of Law—Today," in *Selected Essays on Constitutional Law* (New York: Foundation Press, 1938), I, 311.
37. 110 U.S. 516 (1884).

THE MEANING OF LIBERTY UNDER
THE FOURTEENTH AMENDMENT

The first Justice Harlan argued for a fixed meaning for liberty under due process of law, that is, the provisions of the Bill of Rights. The shorthand approach has in recent years been advanced in minority, principally by Justice Black, who has argued that, otherwise, the judges have excessive freedom to add to or diminish the authority of states to legislate. The prevailing point of view on the Court has emerged from the Twining Case reasoning. "Selective incorporation," has been the order of this century, with the Court gradually, although irreversibly, adding to threshold requirements for upholding state legislation. One by one, the provisions of the Bill of Rights have been held to apply to the states, not in their own right, but as implicit in the Fourteenth Amendment. This dominant approach, as enunciated by Cardozo and Frankfurter most conscientiously and by Harlan, II, most recently, has, for all practical purposes, assimilated the key provisions of Bill of Rights; it is likely that only the requirement of a jury trial, when demanded in suits involving more than $50, will eventually be held not to apply to state legislation. The difference in the selective-incorporation approach, however, is that at least in theory the Justices can withdraw application of a provision, freeing states for its application, as well as adding such requirements. In this sense, Justice Black's criticism of the Twining Case–Cardozo–Frankfurter approach to the Fourteenth Amendment as "the accordion theory" of liberty, by which judges can pump in or press out additional rights, seems justified. Nonetheless, the practical difference between the Harlan I–Black approach and the majority view seems today small and diminishes with every year. By invoking selective incorporation, the majority of the Court bought time, gradually accustoming the states to a situation in which both the content and form of civil liberties were increasingly federalized and made uniform throughout the nation.[38]

Appropriately, First Amendment freedoms were the first to be incorporated. In Gitlow *v.* New York, the Justices laconically noted that "for present purposes we may and do assume that freedom of speech and of the press . . . are among the fundamental personal rights and liberties protected by the due process clause . . . from impairment by the states."[39] At least one authority has suggested that this phrasing was deliberately delphic to cover a possible retreat if needed.[40] But expansion, not contraction, proved the order of the future. Subsequent decisions also indicated the states were bound to observe freedom of religion—both with regard to foregoing establishing of a religion and to protecting its free

---

38. It is usual to think of there being two approaches, but the truth is more complex; there are four, and possibly five, to the problem of incorporation. These are: (1) the total incorporationists of the Black stripe; (2) the total incorporationists who would say all this, plus additional rights, as exemplified by Murphy and Rutledge in the Adamson Case; (3) the selective incorporationists, who then apply those amendments in the same fashion against the states as against the national government; (4) those who insist "incorporation" is a metaphor merely a way of looking at the phrase "due process of law," (for example, Justice Harlan), and not a definition; (5) additionally there is a possible position, perhaps espoused by O. John Rogge, that incorporation should be treated as a legal reality, but more lenient standards should be applied to the states.

It is also usual to act as if the important disagreement was over content, that is, *how much* incorporation. It is increasingly clear that the crucial question is over what happens after incorporation, that is, whether federal standards are to be applied. In our terms, the cutting point comes between approaches 1–3 and 4–5 rather than between 1 and the others. And the single-standard approach is prevailing not only because of a growing sense of national values, but also because the dual standard allows reopening of issues on habeas corpus proceedings or other collateral attack and clogs the federal judicial process.

39. 268 U.S. 652 (1925), p. 666.

40. J. R. Green, "The Bill of Rights, the Fourteenth Amendment and the Supreme Court," in McCloskey, p. 386. Justice Douglas in his oral remarks, Long Island University Conference on the Bill of Rights, December 10, 1966, also suggested Gitlow was more tentative, the case merely seen as having "adumbrated as perhaps it did" include free speech.

exercise—as well as assembly and petition. In 1958, the Court also indicated that a right of association and organization for political expression was also implied in the First Amendment. For all practical purposes, by 1947 it was clear that the entire First Amendment applied to the states.

Further, in spite of the incorporation approach, it also became clear that it was the First Amendment's explicit wording that was being invoked as the standard for dealing with the states. Theoretically, this should not be so, for incorporationists insist that it is the significance of the claimed liberty at stake that brings it within the ambit of the Fourteenth Amendment and that it is the phraseology of the latter that determines constitutionality. The First Amendment presents a particularly strong test for the incorporationist, for its very wording applies to the national level only; it is *Congress* that is forbidden to pass laws abridging the rights enumerated therein. The late Justice Jackson and the present Justice Harlan (whose constitutional views differ from those of his grandfather-namesake by only 180 degrees) have pointed this out emphatically and even eloquently. Not only logic and wording, but also policy considerations, have been urged by these two, who have suggested that the limitations of the Fourteenth Amendment ought to be interpreted less strictly, so that states would have a freer hand in dealing with regulation of expression in keeping with their paramount responsibility for public order. But this double standard—Kalven more neutrally calls it a "two-tiered approach"—has not attracted support. For all practical purposes, the Fourteenth Amendment has, among other accomplishments, altered the legal effect of the First Amendment, so that its wording might just as well be that *Congress and the states* shall make no law affecting religion, the press, speech, and assembly.

Effectively then, too, the problem for the Court for three decades has been finding a uniform definition of the limits of free expression for nation and state, the reconciliation of public order with individual expression for both levels of government. Here, of course, the phenomenon Schubert calls "reverse incorporation" has taken place. And here the historical paucity of litigation and absence of doctrine has made itself felt. Substantively, First Amendment decisions have been a product of the past half-century. Only the past thirty-five years have witnessed invalidation of state laws by means of the complex legerdemain of First Amendment-as-incorporated-in-the-due-process-clause. Even more significantly, invalidation of federal legislation on this basis is a matter almost of days. Not until Lamont *v.* Postmaster, in 1965, was an act of Congress deemed repugnant to free expression. Federal action, however, was invalidated as early as 1943.[41] It has, however, also been common for decades for the courts to construe congressional legislation to avoid questions of constitutionality, a practice that is almost as efficacious—occasionally even more so—than invalidation itself.

GIVING FREEDOM OF SPEECH A MEANING

The history of Supreme Court treatment of free speech, therefore, begins largely with World War I. Prior to that time, the great crises had been resolved in other ways; the Alien and Sedition Acts had been permitted to die a natural death. The anti-incendiary exclusion of Abolitionist materials from the mails, for the most part, had not been legally tested; the rush of events prevented Civil War conflicts from wending their leisurely way through the courts. Neither did the anti-Anarchist waves of the 1890s produce significant legal reaction.

The Supreme Court first faced the problem of depth in the second decade of the twentieth century. In Schenck *v.* United States (1919), Justice Holmes enunciated his "clear

---

41. *Lamont* v. *Postmaster,* 381 U.S. 301 (1965); *Busey* v. *District of Columbia,* 138 F 2d 592 (1943).

and present danger" test as a rule of thumb appropriate for juries in deciding when speech had reached the point of action, in which case it would be punishable. As has been repeatedly pointed out, the rule in its early stages was not utilized as a standard for judging legislation. Yet, by the time of the decision in Whitney *v.* California (1927), Brandeis had no difficulty in invoking the standard as one that defined the limits of legislative action, with agreement by—and no murmurs from—Holmes.

Schenck was eclipsed by Sanford's presentation in Gitlow *v.* New York of the "dangerous tendency" rule, which reduced the question asked by the Court to a mere inquiry into possible effects. For a decade at least, this was the standard used by the Court. Holmes and Brandeis usually concurred in the result, in the light of the circumstances, but were troubled by the reasoning of their colleagues. It was to provide a litmus for the point at which words partook sufficiently of deeds that they—especially Holmes—suggested the "clear and present danger" formula.

The distinction between overt acts and mere opinion was novel, if at all, only to judges. Discussion of such a threshold test dates back to at least the Revolutionary era, although it was generally discussed in the context of religious freedom rather than of free speech generally. Holmes' usage seems to have come from his own celebrated lectures on the common law, where he discussed slander and then immediately generalized a rule for determining causation or liability intents in language remarkably parallel to his later suggestion: "The question in each case is whether the actual choice, or, in other words, the actually contemplated result was near enough to the remoter result complained of to throw the peril of it upon the actor."[42] The historical context in which the two Justices were operating perhaps explains the stickiest problem in the test, the insistence on the judge rather than

---

42. Oliver Wendell Holmes, *The Common Law,* (Boston: Little, Brown & Co., 1881), p. 159.

the jury making the determination of the sufficiency of conditions to justify the limitation of freedom. This was, on the whole, a reversal of historical trends in the common law toward broader jury determination of facts.

With his usual verbal skill, Holmes succeeded in capturing the imagination of professional and lay audiences even as he failed to convince his colleagues. His aphorism, "the most stringent protection of free speech would not protect a man in *falsely* [emphasis added] shouting fire in a theatre," remains a contemporary touchstone in discussions and looms as one of the most misquoted sentences in Bartlett's.

After initial rejection by the majority, "clear and present danger" disappeared from Court discussion only to re-emerge as official doctrine in 1937, employed by a bench upon which neither Holmes nor Brandeis sat. This was the era in which the opinions of the "great dissenters" triumphed generally. Their views, translated into majority doctrine in other areas, however, were to prove more successful than at least the specific formula has been in the free-speech domain.

The triumph of "clear and present danger" is most closely associated with Chief Justice Hughes, who also introduced the closely associated—and still used—technique of voiding restrictive legislation "on its face." His advent to the Court was followed quickly by his decision in Near *v.* Minnesota (1931), which many regard as revitalizing the "clear and present danger" approach, although not repeating those words. But Herndon *v.* Lowry, which came fully six years later, officially embraced the formula.

In practice, the users of "clear and present danger" have experienced severe disappointment. Lack of agreement on its applicability to specific situations and the domain of its appropriateness has been matched by controversy over the outcomes that result. "Clear and present danger," as a consequence, has been criticized as a delusive and empty formula, but it is difficult to see that it is much different from most legal doctrine, that is, it is the starting point rather than the end of discussion in tough cases.

As to its alleged emptiness, Harry Kalven has pointed out that the involuted contortions of the opinions of Frankfurter and Jackson in the Dennis Case attempt to show consistency with Holmes but fail to convince most readers; this, he suggests, indicates the opposite—that "clear and present danger" was a tough instrument blunted by the overexpectations and the ineptitude of its users. But he also suggested that Learned Hand's more complex opinion in The Masses Case—based largely on statutory interpretation—would have put free-speech decisions on a firmer basis.[43] This opinion was apparently shared by Hand, if we may judge by his epitaph for "clear and present danger." In spite of his personal identification with its author, Hand observed, "I cannot help thinking that for once, Homer nodded."[44]

Dissatisfaction developed as special problems—picketing in labor disputes or movie censorship, for example—seemed to present issues extraneous to those implied in "clear and present danger." It was, however, the pyrrhic decision in Dennis *v.* United States that furnished the coup de grâce. At the height of the threat of Communist advances abroad and fear of subversion at home, this appeal of the conviction of first-rung Communist leaders for violation of the Smith Act presented a special dilemma for the Justices. In convicting the Communists, the jury found them guilty of—among other charges—conspiracy to organize to advocate violent overthrow; in short, the government argument was that, in the nature of their structure and ideology, Communist parties are dedicated to attempt overthrow of non-Communist governments when the occasion for such an effort arises. The common sense of the matter is relatively clear, although the presupposition of purity of motivation even among Communists is perhaps exaggerated; the common law also has some problems in proving intentions about future events. But, even assuming the clarity of the danger, what was clear

---

43. Kalven, pp. 13, 37.
44. Learned Hand, *The Bill of Rights* (New York: Atheneum Publishers, 1964), p. 59.

was that it was hardly present or immediate. Chief Justice
Vinson's opinion was firmly based on Learned Hand's Court
of Appeals decision and like it attempted to restate Holmes'
formula to deal with the more comprehensive challenge to
public order; yet, most commentators agree that, in fact,
"clear and present danger" was tortured beyond all recognition. Hand suggested that the formula be expanded to allow
the two elements to compensate for each other; the greater
the danger threatened, the less immediate the threat had to
be. "In each case [they] must ask whether the gravity of the
'evil' discounted by its improbability, justifies such invasion
of free speech as is necessary to avoid the danger,"[45] wrote
Hand, purporting to follow and merely rephrase Holmes.
Where the objective was fundamental—involving the future
of organized society itself—the danger might be remote and
still prohibitable.

Even within the majority camp, Vinson's reasoning left
some aftertaste of dissatisfaction. Frankfurter and Jackson attempted to distinguish subversive organization from expression of opinion. This distinction was later elaborated by such
writers as Sidney Hook and Wallace Mendelson, in suggesting
Communism as a "conspiracy" engaged in "clandestine
speech" was not in "the marketplace of ideas" and not entitled to protection accorded the free exchange of rival
thoughts. This distinction was an indication, as we have
noted, of the compelling character of Holmes' words—and,
even more significantly, of the absence of such convincing
force in Vinson's opinion. Inside and outside the Court, the
conviction grew that the Hand–Vinson formula so completely
blurred the sharp lines of the test as to eliminate it for any
purpose, except apologetic acceptance of all legislative action.

This attitude quickly—by judicial standards at least—
found expression. In Yates *v*. United States, Justice Harlan
deftly resolved the problem, ending the threat seen to free

45.   183 F2d 201 (1950) 212.

expression by a combination of small, technical formulations and a sharp departure from the previous trends. Without referral either to "clear and present danger" or the Hand–Vinson "clear and present danger" approaches, Harlan found that convictions required genuine advocacy or knowing involvement in such actions—standards that on the whole have been found to apply only in singular instances.

Harlan's much-admired opinion in Yates has proved a milestone, for effectively "clear and present danger" has all but disappeared from the Court lexicon. Apparently, the Justices are convinced that the words are unnecessary provocation, a source of heat, with little enough enlightment as a by-product. Nor have they embraced any single formulation, preferring to approach free expression as a complex congeries of different problems rather than a single problem with a universal solvent.

Indeed, during the late 1940s and early 1950s, the Court had also rejected a doctrine developed as a buttress to "clear and present danger," the "preferred freedom" doctrine. We have already examined the general notion of preference, pointing out that, in a loose way, every Justice since 1919 has accepted the notion of additional Court protection for civil liberties. But "preferred freedoms" was a rather catch-all slogan that rallied amorphous forces, which ran from Reed—who seldom voted to invalidate governmental actions—to Murphy, whose sympathies were so prodefendant that lawyers made bad puns about "justice tempered by Murphy." At its zenith, the Black-Douglas-Murphy-Rutledge near-majority pushed the notion that any derogation of personal liberty was presumptively unconstitutional with the burden for sustaining the legislation on the government, reversing the normal presumptions in litigation. Frankfurter, who thought the judiciary ought to scrutinize laws impinging on liberty "with a jealous eye," nonetheless objected vehemently to the notion that the function of the judiciary varied from area to area. The ferocity of his attack on "preferred freedoms"—a doctrine he denounced as "a mischievous phrase," and characterized with at most technical accuracy as having "never commended itself to a majority of this court"—presaged his open espousal of a "balancing" approach to the Bill of Rights.[46] Although a majority of the Justices had—at least if one arrays different opinions and the Justices who had participated in them—endorsed some fairly exact form of "preferred freedoms" prior to Frankfurter's attack in Kovacs *v.* Cooper, the denunciation and the almost simultaneous deaths of Murphy and Rutledge in that same year had an effect similar to that of the Dennis Case on "clear and present danger." An occasional, highly sporadic use of "preferred freedom" language occurred, but, in general, studious avoidance was more common. The notions involved, however, continued to be employed as the Court developed sensitivity to different issues and skill in the development of new techniques to deal with a complex of complex problems.

THE TRANSITORY NATURE OF FREE-SPEECH STANDARDS

The disintegration of the two approaches by which the Court had originally attempted to deal with the central problem of the twentieth century—human freedom—forced the Justices to search more widely, or deeply. Moving from his criticism of preferred weighting, Frankfurter attempted to define a balancing role for the Judges, without quite committing the judiciary to a blank check to the legislature. Justice Black gingerly embraced an absolute position on the First Amendment, at first by indirection, finally even by public non-Court avowal. As these came into collision against a backdrop of older approaches and newer problems, new variations were conceived. Today, Mr. Justice Brennan tells

---

46. But Frankfurter, though his quotations, adroitly conceded his own invocation of the Carolene Products footnote and did not repudiate it.

us that the Court uses at least four approaches in various areas of free expression:

> Each has been primarily utilized to sustain governmental regulation in particular contexts; the "redeeming social value" test primarily in obscenity cases; the "clear and present danger" test primarily in regulation of subversive activity and the "publication of matter thought to obstruct justice," and the "balancing" test primarily in the case of regulations not intended directly to condemn the content of speech, but incidentally limiting its exercise.[47]

Additional ad hoc approaches, trial balloons, and incipient theories have not been lacking. Nor is this surprising; forty years is a relatively short time for constitutional development, especially in so critical an era. It is hardly a source for wonder that the first approaches should have been inadequate. In a recent work, Edward Hudon concludes that, to date, no judicial rule on free expression has managed to survive much more than a decade.[48] Time will tell whether the second-round efforts by the Court will be more successful.

47. William Brennan, "The Supreme Court and the Meiklejohn Interpretation of the First Amendment," *Harvard Law Review*, LXXIX (1965), 11.
48. Edward Hudon, *Freedom of Speech and Press in America* (Washington, D.C.: Public Affairs Press, 1963), p. ix.

3

Constitutional Developments
and Political Freedom

GENERAL CONSIDERATIONS

In theory as well as practice, common-law developments have been slow and organic, accretive rather than sweeping. Courts seldom control the follow-up to their initial decisions, usually having to await further litigation, which is at the discretion of the parties involved and the vagaries of societal evolution. Partly as a consequence of this lack of sustained control, partly because an instinct for institutional protection, and partly because of the general attitude toward legal growth and development, common-law judges work not so much from broad general principles, but usually with more modest and tentative formulations that allow them—or their successors, such is the pace of litigation—

leeway in dealing with overlooked or unanticipated aspects of the subject at hand.

This generally cautious, pragmatic attitude is reinforced in the American tradition of constitutional law, where great issues of statecraft have somewhat artificially been forced into the mold of two-party litigation. Until recently, the British attitude toward basic decisions was nominally that precedents could not be formally reversed, although in practice they might be so "distinguished" as to have no practical effect. Only in 1966 did the Law Lords unexpectedly announce their intention to treat their precedents—like other common-law courts—as normally compelling but not absolutely binding. The United States Supreme Court early recognized the difficulties that would be created by the acceptance of the attitude of irrevocability said to have been adopted by the Medes and Persians in dealing with the gutsy issue of governmental power: "It is a constitution we are expounding," as Marshall neatly summarized the situation. In basic areas—for example, the commerce clause—there has been an avoidance of sweeping programs and often the coexistence of rival and even contradictory doctrines used by the Court in day-to-day resolution of cases. Even in the modern era, since 1937, when earlier confusion became so rampant as to compel a housecleaning, some clearly illogical elements are still maintained. The Court, for example, maintains that its authority over interstate barriers emanates from the negative implications of the Commerce Clause itself, but it defers to congressional authorization of state legislation that it finds otherwise forbidden by the Constitution; Congress can permit something that is constitutionally impermissible. No great effort is made to reconcile these diverse assertions inasmuch as the basic resulting pattern seems to satisfy the equally diverse governmental and economic needs involved. The system is somewhat untidy, but workable.

The emergence of free expression as a central issue for our society has presented the Court with a problem analogous to that of finding standards for commerce-clause litigation. As we have already observed, the task has already proved a difficult one, and some standards have already been found outmoded; others have been tried as comprehensive tests only to be relegated to more limited tasks—something like a newly-wed who tries to prepare all meals with a pressure cooker and slowly comes to the conclusion that it is chiefly useful with a small number of items requiring long simmering. Still others have been pressed only in dissent, and therefore never really tested, or discussed only as possibilities even by their sponsors. On the other hand, some doctrines have been adopted without extended discussion of their implications. Particularly during the period in which Chief Justice Stone presided (1941–1946), a good deal of very explicit discussion of basic issues and broad general principles emerged in every decision. The result seemed to be to multiply many differences without much reason. Perhaps as a consequence of this, no doubt also reflecting different personalities on today's Court, the current Justices have muted some of these broad differences and have adhered more strictly to the cases at hand. Although much more candid about the true issues or policy considerations of decision than the pre-1940 Court, the present bench relies less on sweeping formula than the Stone Court. The problems of the past have shaped the discretion of the present.[1]

STANDARDS OF FREE EXPRESSION: ABSOLUTISM

The official and prevailing attitude of the Court remains the balancing test, although it is clear that elements of absolutism are being absorbed, that "preferred freedoms" is by no means rejected—except as a name, and that aspects of

---

1. An unfortunate exception can apparently be found in the decisions on legislative investigations, where sweeping and rather banal judgments seem to prevail and radical shifts in decision have been common.

still other approaches have been specifically adapted to deal with specified limited problems. Thus, although nominally the Frankfurter argument for balancing has prevailed, the one sure generalization is that it has largely been rejected. On the other hand, the thrust of Frankfurter's campaign against efforts to rely on a single formula has been at least partially successful.

Current discussion on the Court now centers on the relative merits of absolutism and balancing. Both doctrinal viewpoints are closely attached to, and can be regarded as derivative from, more fundamental attitudes toward the judicial process. Both labels are highly and accurately descriptive of what is entailed. Yet, as usual with any shorthand description, when the label is pierced, additional problems with both notions and some reconciliation of the two approaches emerge. As works of art, the labels are no more successful than most.

The absolutist approach—still a minority one—seems, on the surface, the simplest. It is, of course, the literalist approach as well in the hands of Mr. Justice Black. "I understand that it is rather old-fashioned and shows a slight naivete to say that 'no law' means 'no law.' " "It is my belief that there are 'absolutes' in our Bill of Rights, and that they were put there on purpose by men who knew what words meant. . . ."[2]

Its justification was rather more complex as Meiklejohn formulated it. Free speech was to be protected for utilitarian social reasons. Speech not clearly directed toward an informational function was not equally protected. This dichotomization of speech into "community thinking process" and other merely private speech Meiklejohn saw as having constitutional counterparts. Political speech, that necessary for an

---

2. "Justice Black and First Amendment Absolutes: A Public Interview," *NYU Law Review*, XXXVI (1962), 573; Hugo Black, "The Bill of Rights," in Edmond Cahn (ed.), *The Great Rights* (New York: The Macmillan Co., 1963), p. 45.

enlightened electorate, was First Amendment speech, with a first-class absolute ticket. Other discussion—personal gossip, childish prattle, light entertainment—was in another, less plush, category.[3] Its protection was embodied in the Fifth Amendment, which allows restrictions on liberty providing only that there is due process of law. (The Fourteenth Amendment, in turn, controls state action and requires that state governments meet the federal standards for the two types of self-expression.) Thus Meiklejohn saw libel laws as permissible and at a minimum left ambiguous the problem of obscenity and other moral censorship.

Indeed, this division into types of speech evoked immediate criticism. Chafee, for example, suggested Meiklejohn's approach seemed to justify censorship for all theater and art and that academic freedom was in a subordinate, Fifth Amendment category. In revising his slender seminal volume, Meiklejohn went to considerable pains to indicate his espousal of blue-ribbon treatment for academics and artists but thereby exposed the lack of any real guidance except intuition in demarcating the two types of expression.[4] Even on its own terms, Meiklejohn's approach was badly flawed.

Justice Black's espousal of absolutism was anything but precipitate; rather, he seems to have cautiously debated with himself, cryptically hinted at his approach in opinions, perhaps allowed a former law clerk to reveal his attitude, used extremely broad language in dissents (where broad generalizations are not necessarily taken at face value)—all these before openly stating his acceptance of the doctrine. It is therefore not surprising to find that his absolutism is anything but a slavish imitation of Meiklejohn's. To date at least, he has avoided open acceptance of the philosopher's

---

3. Alexander Meiklejohn, *Political Freedom* (New York: Oxford University Press, 1960), esp. pp. 25–9 and chap. xv.
4. Chafee, Book Review, *Harvard Law Review*, LXII (1949), 891; Meiklejohn, *Political Freedom*, pp. 124–31 and 145–6; and "The First Amendment Is an Absolute," *The Supreme Court Review*, (1961), 256–7.

division of areas of free speech, although he has followed an older legal doctrine, the exclusion of some forms of speech from the First Amendment. Even before embracing absolutism, Black had, with the rest of the Court, accepted the "fighting words" doctrine of the Chaplinsky Case—that a volley of swear words constitutes something less than free expression—and the Thornhill doctrine on mass picketing—that arraying large numbers of demonstrators with intimidating force was something more than speech. Thus, he excludes some matters from First Amendment protection; but it would appear that he rejected the notion of Fifth Amendment speech. He has not directly said so, but his failure to seize opportunities to state this portion of Meiklejohn's approach and the surface incompatibility with other Black ideas suggest rejection. It hardly seems possible now to spell out such a position without embarrassment, particularly for a Justice who has made so much in his judicial program of denouncing "sky's the limit" judicial control through such concepts as due process.

Whether or not Black's avoidance of a two-category approach to free speech constitutes a departure, it seems clear that his formulation is more emphatic and consistent than Meiklejohn's. This is revealed in his well-publicized attitudes on libel. Nothing could more dramatically set off Black's attitude than his denial of the constitutionality of libel suits in a public interview with Edmond Cahn and the almost simultaneous statement by Meiklejohn that "in cases of private defamation . . . the First Amendment gives no protection to the person sued. His verbal attack has no relation to the business of governing."[5] More recently, Harry Kalven has suggested that Black may have been misunderstood. "The interview is not a great success and I find it difficult to say how far Justice Black was carrying his opposition. . . . His answer is primarily about federal law."[6] One must concede

---

5. Meiklejohn, "The First Amendment Is an Absolute," p. 259.
6. Kalven, p. 52.

that the statements might be more graceful, yet they are hardly so murky:

> I do not hesitate, so far as my own view is concerned, as to what should be and what I hope will sometime be the constitutional doctrine that just as it was not intended to authorize damage suits for mere words as distinguished from conduct as far as the federal government is concerned, the same rule should apply to the states.[7]

Black's position seems clear. The First Amendment, in his view, prohibited any libel suits in federal courts. He seems less convinced—but nonetheless affirms—that the framers of the Fourteenth Amendment intended to restrict the states and seems to be advocating or prophesying a period of gradual acceptance of such an abolition—gradual either because he expects judicial reluctance or for policy reasons to allow society to adjust to the change.

So Black has generally attempted to meet and deal with what is perhaps the most glaring weakness in the Meiklejohn approach—the almost total absence of an historical base for a utilitarian absolutism, modified though it be by Meiklejohn's qualification through classification. Although there is considerable history to suggest that the notion of political freedom was quite well understood and established, the complex separation of types of discourse does not appear to have been articulated in the constitutional period. Black's absolutism seems closer to the discussion by, among others, Brant, which suggests that federal considerations as well as libertarian ones shaped the First Amendment, and this is seen as totally excluding national regulation of expression.[8] This view reduces the problem to the narrower one of application of the

---

7. Black, "A Public Interview," p. 578.
8. Irving Brant, "Seditious Libel: Myth and Reality," *New York University Law Review*, XXXIX (1964) 1.

Fourteenth Amendment, an issue that presents difficulties for more orthodox historical interpreters as well.

APPLYING STANDARDS: ABSOLUTISM

But Black has not solved the problem of defining the outer limits of application of the First Amendment, the extent to which regulation in the name of other portions of the Constitution may impinge on free expression. As critics— sometimes also friends—delight in pointing out, Black, at the point of defining boundaries, must in fact balance considerations of social policy. Inferentially and overtly as well, Black has conceded this, and his criticism is of ad hoc balancing. He is not critical of what he regards as a legitimate judicial function of defining the fixed perimeters of legitimate governmental power, where the judge distinguishes, say, between the relative social interest in free expression lost by limiting mass picketing and the eminently greater threat of social intimidation if regulation is forbidden. He finds offensive, however, the judicial approach that attempts to bring into play all immediate conditions, to evaluate the social interest in the contested legislation. Black regards this as doubly offensive. First, it projects the Court into dealing with matters as would a legislature; second, it effectively eliminates the First Amendment as a genuine limit, for, in the heat of the moment, judges are likely to be influenced by the same forces that originally caused passage of restrictive legislation. Instead of dealing dispassionately with distribution of power, in relatively objective and even timeless fashion, judges are forced by the balancing approach—in Black's view at least— to act in consonance with the shifting tides of popular opinion. So, Black argues, his absolutism is truer to the normal judicial function, whereas the balancing approach is Aesopian language for acquiescence in total legislative discretion. The most comprehensive use of quasi-Meiklejohnian reasoning by the Court majority to date has occurred in the field of obscenity, although a diluted form applied in the area of libel can be regarded as the greatest triumph in practical terms. With regard to obscenity, the Supreme Court has held exclusively prurient materials to be outside the protection of the First Amendment, a result that can be justified either in Meiklejohn's terms or in the older "fighting words" doctrine. But this demarcation, at first sight a restriction of expression, became the cornerstone of greater permissiveness as offsetting criteria of social worth were added to the picture. Instead of such single-factor formulae as "hard-core pornography," which attempted to distinguish the motivation of the artist from that of the pornographers by evaluating the product, a threefold test emerged from the Ginzburg and *Fanny Hill* Cases, the degree of prurience "being utterly without redeeming social value" and the indicae of purpose derived from the method of distribution. The social effect, particularly of the last test, was to move the focus of control from content to means of promotion. The effect was to all but abandon control over the determined consumer—the hard core pornographee, so to speak—but limit access to a wider, younger, and presumably more pliable audience through control of the type of distribution. It is interesting that, in an era in which frank discussion of policy reasons is the mode, no such discussion took place in this important instance.

At first sight, these principles have little to do with absolutism. Certainly, there is no necessary derivation, and inspection reveals current efforts to be a marriage of Meiklejohn's notions, balancing (the Ginzburg calculus smacks of Hand's "clear and probable" discounting), and older ad hoc doctrines like the Chaplinsky "fighting words" decision. Black and Douglas also argue, usually in dissent, that an absolute interpretation of the First Amendment requires striking down all efforts to regulate pornography. But Justice Brennan, the Court's chief spokesman in such matters, has acknowledged his own indebtedness and Meiklejohn's primary influence in the obscenity area.[9]

Similarly, it has been Brennan rather than Black who has been the spokesman in the less sweeping emergence of new constitutional prohibitions on libel suits and who has fashioned more tentative, pragmatic, and flexible standards with limits that can be adjusted by time, experience, and case-by-case litigation. The backdrop for such a development occurred when, in Barr *v.* Matteo,[10] the Court made explicit what previous decisions had indicated, that a federal official who issues a statement arising in the course of his duties is immune from libel suits. (As the Attorney General quickly warned officials and reassured the public, the indicated standard—arising from duty—was a formidable limit on irresponsible and malicious statements.) Still, if the official could comment on the citizen without financial risk, who could doubt a reciprocal immunity was in the offing?

The opportunity for such legal breakthrough presented itself in a case that actually demanded novel treatment if the "sense of justice" was to be satisfied. An Alabama jury had awarded a tidy $500,000 damages against the *New York Times* for publishing an advertisement containing criticism, and some misstatements of fact, about public officials, including by inference Police Commissioner "Bull" Connor who was involved in racial troubles in Birmingham. The jury apparently evaluated the potency of the *Times* highly, for, in spite of the somewhat limited circulation of that publication in Alabama (394), the verdict was several times higher than any previous libel verdict recorded in that state—$45,000. This award was all the more remarkable in the fact of the genuine ambiguity in the identity of the officials being criticized and the improbability of any damage to reputation aris-

---

9. *Ginzburg* v. *United States,* 383 U.S. 463 (1966); Brennan, "The Supreme Court and the Meiklejohn Interpretation of the First Amendment," p. 1.
10. 360 U.S. 564 (1959).

ing from the inaccuracies in a state generally favoring the officials' activities anyway. It was clear that what was involved here was a southern jury's revenge on northern "foreign imperialist" journalists, who so often had assumed the right to lecture their region on just this topic, the handling of the South's peculiar problem. But the weapon they were forging was an awesome one, suggesting that public officials with local popular support sufficient to promise a favorable jury verdict could be criticized only at the risk of award of stupendous sums unrelated to any real evaluation of damages.

In the *Times* Case, the Court made symmetrical the immunity granted officials by outlawing libel suits by such officials against citizen critics, except where "malice" (reckless disregard for the truth) is shown. In Barr *v.* Matteo, the utility of frank governmental pronouncements and the need to protect public officials from frittering away their time in protecting themselves from litigation had been evaluated as of greater significance than the individual interest in vindication and damages. In the *Times* Case, the individual citizen's sovereign right to chastize his public employees was seen as more valuable and deserving of protection than the official's right to initiate litigation. This immunity from suit was an intensification of the "fair comment" rule with regard to public officials—a rule of long standing, which was originally established on much the same reasoning. (Incidentally, in both instances, balancing was necessary to establish results that could be regarded as absolute in origin.) Further litigation is testing the limits of the exemption—for example, whether individuals who enter the "vortex of political controversy" expose themselves to the same scope of comment as those in formal positions. Certainly, this represents a legal development that might not have occurred without the impetus of Meiklejohn's little volume.

Already, however, we have also had some rather definite evidence of the limits of the absolute approach as well as its triumphs. In sustaining government authority, the absolute approach provides little if any guidance. This problem is rooted in Meiklejohn's writings, where he disposes of the problem largely by means of simple analogy, dear to the heart of any philosophy professor but not necessarily adequate for disposing of complex social confrontations. First Amendment speech can be abridged, Meiklejohn says,

> . . . only in the social situation, which for the time renders the community incapable of the reasonable consideration of the issues of policy which confront it. . . . When the roof falls in, a moderator may, without violating the First Amendment, declare the meeting adjourned.[11]

In essence, this suggests that there are limits in time and place for free expression, but that fact was generally appreciated even prior to iteration of the analogy. It is, of course, important and necessary that Meiklejohn inform us that his approach does not preclude reasonable regulation of the flow of expression, but he gives us no guidelines for testing such reasonableness. "Some absolutes," Professor Karst has observed acidly, "are thus equipped with elastic boundaries."[12]

All too often, the outcome in free-speech and free-press cases hinges on the simple question largely avoided here: When is an exercise of governmental authority in denial of the right of expression an impermissible invasion of individual rights—rights that are to be defended as buttressing the public good—and when is such exercise a necessary measure for public safety? Even the greatest tyrant seldom asserts—and probably is unwise to ever assert—that a restriction is instituted for its own sake; *sic volo, sic jubeo*. Only in fiction and even then, only in the privacy of Orwell's *1984* torture cells) do rulers sadistically demand that one see five fingers when four are really in evidence simply for the sake

11.   Meiklejohn, *Political Freedom*, p. 49.
12.   Kenneth Karst, "Legislative Facts in Constitutional Litigation," *Supreme Court Review*, LXXV (1960), 79.

of ratifying their own sense of power. In real life, assertion of power is cloaked in pleas of altruism and necessity: "We are compelled to stop the speaker for he is threatening the peace of the community."

In this respect, the Feiner Case[13] is almost the epitome of the total problem, with a policeman trying to make a good-faith, on-the-spot decision also caught in the dilemma of authority. In this case, as in the Jehovah's Witnesses prose-lyting cases—testing licensing, prohibition of leaflet distribu-tion, and limitations on decibels of sound, among other problems—and the recent causes involving civil-rights dem-onstrations, the essential problem has been in defining the proper mode—the time, place, and manner of peaceful peti-tioning—and not the content per se.

Here, as in many instances, regulations of circumstances could easily dominate content. If the authorities may sweep expression under the rug away from public attention, they can effectively repress without official suppression. No one advocates the right to say anything, anytime, anywhere. One who speaks in monolithic terms, therefore, has special prob-lems in defining spheres of authority, or his absolutism be-comes a veneer, like the ringing guarantees of free expression in the Soviet constitution. Meiklejohn's heroic effort to dis-tinguish spheres of expression, helpful enough in the sphere of aesthetic literature, provides virtually no help at all where a genuinely valuable social discussion threatens to explode into violence.

So, unexpectedly but not inconsistently, Justice Black parts company with his liberal conferees on the Court on the issue of the sit-ins and other demonstrations. Holding para-mount the right of private property, Black has little difficulty where trespass is the issue. Indeed, even his colleagues gen-erally assent that one may not generally compel use of another's property for free-speech purposes, and they justify

---

13. *Feiner* v. *New York*, 340 U.S. 315 (1951).

the demonstrators usually by finding state intervention where Black—and usually Harlan, White, and Clark—could find none. But, what of public demonstrations in public facilities? Black insists on limits but states them without reference to any articulated decision rules, let alone absolutes. The majority (and Black's most consistent partner over the years, Douglas) has conversely been reaching its more sweeping conclusions without reference to absolutes, which, it becomes evident, are in essence statements of conclusions, rather than a method of arriving at the decision.

On net, it is difficult to see the absolute formula as one of Black's most happy judicial efforts. The motivations and temptations for him to accept the doctrine are clear, and some accomplishments clearly can be attributed to the formula. But, on close analysis, it is a "mischievous phrase" that confounds its users; it is the fire to the "clear and present danger" frying pan. It is precisely its most vigorous espousers who have had the most difficulty with absolutism.

Black moved to absolutism under extreme pressure, and it is a tribute both to his craftsmanship and statesmanlike instincts that he turned to this view slowly and carefully and with apparent appreciation of its limitations. He turned to it at the time of decline in libertarian fortunes. In the nation, an intolerance born of foreign conflict tested our commitment to freedom of expression, while on the Court the deaths only a few months apart of Murphy and Rutledge sadly depleted judicial opposition to restrictive legislation. The language of absolutism was particularly useful in dissent, a rallying cry and even a convenient shibboleth. But when more affirmative exposition must be made, it is a less opaque position. No doubt Black recognized this, for, shortly after a majority of the Court explicitly repudiated absolutism in the 1961 Koningsberg decision, he made an unusual public exposition of his free-speech position, followed a year later by another in the form of a public interview with the late Edmond Cahn.

As early as the Koningsberg decision, Black conceded that "weighing of the circumstances" was a proper test in evaluating legislation based on a proper governmental interest, which was not a direct regulation of the content of expression but which, incidentally, had a curtailing effect on the possible circumstances of expression. This concession has essentially been reiterated in the Barenblatt, Cox, and Courthouse Trespass cases:

> The First and Fourteenth Amendments, I think, take away from government, state and federal, all power to restrict freedom of speech, press, and assembly *where people have a right to be for such purposes.* . . . Picketing, though it may be utilized to communicate ideas, is not speech, and therefore is not of itself protected by the First Amendment.[14]

What the Justice then means by absolutism is something less sweeping than many off the Court—and quite probably also on—have imagined. It is constancy in time and circumstance that is the major quest in Black's effort. Although it has the more obvious meaning that no direct infringement on the content of expression is permissible, the real equivalent of Black's use of "absolute" is "consistent" or "definite." (One is tempted to say "eternal.") The question of whether some type of regulation is permissible is a generalized question involving broad issues, not a particularized and detailed legislative weighing of circumstances. If it is a permissible regulation, the easing of the cold war or the attitude of Congress is irrelevant. If forbidden infringement is involved, the strength of the Communist Party is irrelevant. It is decision by definition, rather than by balancing, that Black seeks.

But neither definition nor weighing is intrinsically either libertarian or restrictive. It is its application that is significant. To date, we have had little explanation of how we distinguish indirect from direct violations of expression,

---

14.   *Cox v. Louisiana,* 379 U.S. 536, 559 (1965), p. 578.

which, in Black's terms, determines which test would apply. The essence of the majority opinion in Dennis *v.* United States, as in the Douds Case, was that it was a punishment of conspiracy and organization—that is, an indirect curtailment of expression. More than a semantic differentiation between expression and action will be necessary if the test is to prevail. But it would appear from Black's efforts that he weighs to validate legislation and invokes absolutes to invalidate. That is, his tests are indeed concealed conclusions rather than methods of arriving at a decision.

STANDARDS OF DECISION: BALANCING

On the other hand, the balancing approach is, by definition, a triumph of method over content. In essence, it is a negative statement suggesting lack of differentiation of Bill of Rights matters from other judicial matters, but it offers no explanation of the consequences of the emphatic wording of the Bill of Rights provisions or of broad and enduring attitudes on the primacy of human rights over property rights. In short, it asserts in broad terms what each Justice embracing the approach denies to a greater or lesser extent in his actual decision-making—that is, it asserts that civil-liberties decisions are relatively ad hoc balances, say, like water-rights cases, with no really enduring principles involved.

On inspection of its historical antecedents, the curious adequacy of balancing becomes understandable. It was articulated by Frankfurter precisely as a defensive or critical stance vis-à-vis, first, "preferred freedoms" and, later, absolutism. As such, it was intended more to cure what Frankfurter saw as excesses than to formulate positive standards. Further, Frankfurter saw the lessons of history and the innate craftsmanship of the good Justice as supplying the content for the values employed in decision-making, here as in most other areas of jurisprudence. Therefore, he, unlike Black, who sternly seeks to minimize such values, felt no need to supply decision rules for Justices; in his view, they should bring to bear instead their most valuable asset, their decision sense.

There are thus numerous results possible, all consistent with balancing, particularly since there is no consistency of approach or definition of what is being balanced against what. Frankfurter himself, as Harry Kalven has shown, used radically different calculations in quite similar types of case. The possible variations become that much greater if one moves from one Justice to another. The result, it has been suggested, is that whichever Justice is making the decision has been far more critical than whatever test he is applying. Charles Black, who makes this point, suggests that the type of test used is merely a good index to the psychological predispositions of the Justices—less libertarian Justices are attracted to the weaker language of balancing—rather than an ultimate determinant of decision.

Indeed, it has been argued that the term is designed to hide the fact that civil liberties are, through judicial legerdemain, being made residual, or secondary. In this view, values can only be arrayed in a hierarchy, and the notion of balancing disguises the essence of choosing from one value or another—perhaps with deliberate intent on the part of the judges:

> Often an attempt is made to obscure this fact by calling adjudication a "balancing" process. This implies that the competing values are commensurable, that they can be compared as unequal quantities of like units, so that judicial decision is merely the determination of the greater and the less. In fact, of course, the opposed values are always qualitatively different; and the judge—or legislator—who believes that he has placed the responsibility for choice upon a scale merely deludes himself. One wonders, of course, whether anyone really deludes himself in this way.[15]

15. Francis D. Wormuth and Harris G. Mirkin, "The Doctrine of the Reasonable Alternative," *Utah Law Review*, IX (1964), 255.

It is difficult to state much precisely about the pattern of human thought, both because of the state of development of psychology and the ambiguity of the term "values," which can usually be indefinitely redefined into more precise choice statements. But it would appear from what we do know that, in an imprecise and confusing way, "balancing" is a more accurate description of choice than the over-rationalistic approach suggested by Wormuth and Mirkin. Indeed, it is probable that intuitively judges make a judgment in which incommensurable values are somehow evaluated, and the judgments are then rationalized or explained in the hierarchical terms that Wormuth and Mirkin believe to be the mode of decision. How, in fact, in particular situations individuals balance gain and risk, aesthetics and morals, stress and ambition, is one of the greater mysteries of human personality.

Although a purely intuitive translation of different values into some decision calculus is permissible for one's own personal choices, any public decision-maker must make the process more overt; hunch yields to computer simulation in the Department of Defense—and progressively. A judge who must justify a broader range of choice with a broader proliferation of alternatives over an indefinite period of time seldom, therefore, can truly elaborate his process. Indeed, because of the difficulty of such delineation, he may resort to statements based on principle, which in no sense defines his process of choice and may be no guide to future choices but conforms to the expectations of the judicial process. At its best, the balancing approach attempts to get a judge to set forth his considerations—whether hierarchical or scaled— and as such could contribute to a fuller and more candid discussion.

But the problem is not in its ideal terms but in its application, which seldom approximates any level of useful candor. The problem does not appear to be, as Wormuth and Mirkin believe, that balancing is a false description and prescription. Rather, it seems to be so general as to be almost empty and therefore of little utility in either capacity. In a sense, there are as many balancing approaches as there are Justices.

APPLYING STANDARDS: BALANCING

There is, however, a central difference between types of balancing. On the one hand, there is balancing of relatively fundamental considerations—say, in deciding whether an area was subject to regulation, the laying down of broad classes of factors to be weighed against one another—and, on the other, weighing specific circumstances and considerations of the moment, referred to by some writers as ad hoc balancing.

The first type is, in fact, a description of the judicial function per se. It is in essence inescapable. When Black finds that civil-rights demonstrations have exceeded their bounds, he is evaluating the interests of Negroes—and the community—in the right to demonstrate and in achieving gains against the interest of all in law and order. Whatever formula he uses, he must *evaluate,* which, if dictionaries are not deceiving, is a process of balancing.

Ad hoc balancing, on the other hand, seems to be the usual result of acceptance of the balancing formula as an official standard (not that any Justice overtly embraces such a process or endorses it). The rationale for balancing is always in terms of the broader judicial function, in denial of some other formula that will dispose of the matter automatically. But, in practice, the very use of the wording seems to push toward considerations that are neither far-reaching nor persuasive. Indeed, all too often, they involve matters—such as current political tensions and attitudes—not clearly capable of judicial evaluation at all. The nub of the problem has tended to be the proper deference to be paid to legislative findings. Since Congress has acted, it generally has done so after striking a balance of interests of its own. The standards applied with respect to other legislation, of deference to legislators, would virtually amount to accepting the Learned Hand position that the Bill of Rights is in fact a set of guidelines to Congress rather than judicially enforceable provisions. "Above all," a vigorous defender of balancing has argued, "the open balancing technique is calculated to leave 'the sovereign prerogative of choice' to the people—with the least interference that is compatible with our tradition of judicial review."[16] Particularly when dealing with congressional action, balancing involves greater respect for legislative action; to a large extent, indeed, balancers assume that the action of legislators is identical with the will of the majority.

The problems of applying the balancing technique are manifold, particularly in the absence of guidelines. Thus, in attempting to testify on the district-court level in the Barenblatt Case, Thomas Emerson, a most precise and knowledgeable writer on the First Amendment, set forth a host of considerations that might be balanced—the long-range legal power of Congress, the strength of the Communist Party, Barenblatt's personal situation, and a host of other matters. After several hours, he had merely sketched the beginnings of his inquiry, and the judge prudently refused to accept Emerson's inquiry into balancing as evidence.[17]

Inevitably, too, judges have fallen afoul of a trap pointed out by Roscoe Pound early in the century. When dealing with interests, it is possible to analyze the consideration in terms of individuals or, more abstractly, of groups and other social entities. Although either is permissible and, indeed, most of the time we do no violence to realities by speaking on two levels, we take the risk of distortion when we intermix them.

---

16. Wallace Mendelson, "On the Meaning of the First Amendment: Absolutes in the Balance," p. 826.
17. Thomas Emerson, "The First Amendment: What Factors Should Be Considered in Striking the Balance Under Barenblatt," *Law Guild Review,* XX, (1960), 41.

When the balancing on free-speech cases is done, as is unfortunately normal, in terms of individual rights on the one hand and social benefits on the other, the resultant decision is all but foredoomed. It is the dilemma posed by Hand's formula in the Dennis Case all over. If it is the right of existence of the body politic that is at stake as against the sacrifice of a portion of the privilege of a small group, who would not preserve the basic institution essential to the existence of rights? This form of balance tips the scales. More appropriately, the consideration should be at the same level of analysis. A fairer balance is struck by comparing either the individual net gain in security against a loss in free expression or the societal stake in free speech as against the presumed augmentation of security. Even so, the inherent human tendency is to blanch at risk, particularly when framed in terms of societal survival as one of the stakes. Invisibly, an immense weight is added to the scales. Presumably, it was to counteract this, to provide a long-term perspective and an historical judgment in favor of avoidance of regulation, that the federal—and state—Bills of Rights were formulated. Clearly, it is to counteract this tendency that balancing is opposed by its critics.

Difficulties in ascertaining what is being balanced are only part of the story. Even Justice Frankfurter found it hard to be consistent in his statement of what balance was to be struck in order to achieve which result. This variation has led Harry Kalven to observe: "It is clear, I think, that the technique of balancing has not yet been perfected as an analytic tool; it appears to change from case to case."[18]

In the Beauharnais Case, Frankfurter suggested that the legislature had the same broad authority in matters of discourse as in economic process cases, where there had been no invalidations since 1937. Legislation was to be upheld unless the statute was "a willfull and purposeless regulation unrelated to the peace and well-being of the state."[19] Statements

---

18. Kalven, p. 104.
19. *Beauharnais* v. *Illinois*, 343 U.S. 250 (1952), p. 258.

such as this were used by Frankfurter's critics to suggest that he actually put the commerce clause in a preferred position and relegated the First Amendment to a most minor role indeed, for Frankfurter saw a major role for the judiciary in striking down state laws detrimental to interstate commerce.

Yet, in the Sweezy Case, Frankfurter suggested quite a different balancing standard—"a subordinating interest that is controlling." Now, a compelling interest would clearly be within the ambit of rationality, but the obverse is not necessarily true. Programs can fail to reflect a subordinating interest without being clearly irrational. Further, Frankfurter compounded the problem by suggesting in such cases as Shelton *v.* Tucker that, if *any* proper motive for the legislature can be imagined, the legislation is to be upheld.[20] There is, in fact, a difference between these standards that is not only not trivial, but rather at least as profound as that between the principal groups in the Court.

And these tests are in fact still used by the chief remaining exponents of balancing on the Court, most notably Justice Harlan. It would appear that the acid tests for a judge using the absolute approach comes when sustaining governmental power, whereas a judge using the balancing test is least at ease and must invent new approaches when invalidating legislation. Kalven's point, then, seems well taken; balancing is a shifting test that needs honing.

The very indefiniteness of the basic approach, however, is a source of strength, for balancing is the more nonexclusive standard that can accommodate and incorporate others. Like Confucianism and Buddhism, its permeability can be an asset in any long-range test of survival. There seems to be no need to repudiate balancing while adopting a more stringent rule in some areas. Thus, after the *New York Times* decision, Kalven suggested a sweeping shift had taken place repudiating most of the subsidiary rules. Justice Brennan,

---

20. See Kalven, pp. 102–6.

although conceding and even enhancing the significance of the *Times* decision—as well as Meiklejohn's contribution—warned about over-generalizing and exaggerating the sweep of change in doctrine: "Of course if Professor Kalven is right, this is an event of considerable importance. . . . But a caveat is in order. Radical shifts in judicial doctrine are rare. They usually occur over long periods, step-by-step."[21] To date at least, the Justice's information has proven more accurate than textual inference, which is perhaps as it should be. Indeed, in the Garrison Case, he helped vindicate his own prediction by citing both Roth and Beauharnais, thus emphasizing doctrinal continuity. More than that, Brennan's delineation of functional use of rules indicates, too, the greater catholicity of the balancing test. Being as generic as it is, secondary tests are not only compatible, but even necessary. Absolutism (or something else) in libel of public officials, social value in obscenity, "clear and present danger" in small, face-to-face situations—these and more can all be encompassed within one approach.

THE MELDING OF STANDARDS

Because absolutism is a jealous god, it would seem that balancing as a general approach, with special inputs in various areas, would have a practical appeal to judges who have learned by experience how little sweeping standards resolve complex matters. This seems particularly persuasive when it is realized that absolutism can be absorbed and utilized in those areas in which experience suggests its appropriateness, whereas balancing can be explicitly ad hoc in new, untried, and/or uncertain and highly volatile areas. Something like the process of incorporation under the Fourteenth Amendment can take place at a rate and to the degree deemed desirable by the Justices. "The Court's interminable processes

---

21. Brennan, p. 10.

of exclusion and inclusion" of this type is usually favored, for it can be described as the judicial equivalent of eating one's cake and having it, too. Even judges generally find such a prospect irresistible.

The results have been consistent with this speculation. Where balancing has been too vague a method to deal with consistently pressing questions—most conspicuously, in dealing with obscenity—the Justices have sought additional criteria. Where experience had already suggested they could easily do so, as in seditious libel, they have tipped the balance a bit more absolutely, while preserving the requirement that the writer not act in consciousness of falsehood or with malice. On the other hand, in dealing with delicate matters impinging on the prerogatives of Congress—such as investigations or the fundamental need to preserve public safety—they have clung to balancing. Indeed, Justice Brennan suggests strongly that it will remain the official—even nominal—test on such matters for some time and that, if it in fact is displaced, it will be a gradual rather than precipitate change.

JUDICIAL STANDARDS: "PREFERRED FREEDOMS"

The phrase "preferred freedoms" has a precise origin. It was first used by Stone, in dissent, in Jones v. Opelika, a case that signalled a temporary crystallization of a libertarian majority when the initial decision was reversed on rehearing.[22] In Murdock v. Pennsylvania, Rutledge embraced the term and thus initiated a phase of constitutional discussion unusually bitter and in many ways unique.

In contrast, the doctrine, like Topsy, evolved in amorphous ways and never settled down to even a core of meaning. Drawing part of its inspiration from Cardozo's observation in Palko v. Connecticut that basic liberties constitute the

---

22. *Jones* v. *Opelika,* 316 U.S. 584, 608, (1962); reversed on rehearing, 319 U.S. 103 (1943).

"matrix" of democratic society, the liberal wing of the Court insisted on the need for special protection of First Amendment freedoms. At times, the argument for this extra protection merely invoked the need for some added bonus to be put in the scales of judicial decision; Pritchett compares this to "the butcher who consistently weighs his thumb along with the meat."[23] However, although it was never precisely articulated, the suggestion, at other times, seemed to be that laws in any way abridging basic freedoms were to be presumed unconstitutional, and the burden of proof was to be on the government to justify its action.

Against this position, Frankfurter and Jackson, in particular, were to wage unrelenting and vociferous warfare in their decisions. They bitterly warned against "formulistic solutions" that would bring about the same fate for civil liberties as had been brought about for constitutional laissez faire, "which was discredited by being overdone."[24]

The peculiar plasticity of the "preferred freedoms" approach is such that it is difficult to know whether Jackson's sallies were indeed appropriate. Furthermore, rightly or wrongly, Frankfurter and Jackson were convinced that the label masked something quite different, "a novel, iron constitutional doctrine," clearly the views of Meiklejohn.[25] The liberal majority of the early 1940s was peculiarly unable to state its intentions unequivocally.

Certainly, there was considerable tugging and pulling within the "preferred freedoms" camp, so that lack of a durable majority was a major cause of uncertain and unstable doctrine. As Frankfurter pointed out, there was no single opinion using both the approach and phrase that secured a

23. C. Herman Pritchett, *Civil Liberties and the Vinson Court* (Chicago: University of Chicago Press, 1954), p. 249.
24. Jackson in *Douglas* v. *City of Jeannette*, 319 U.S. 157 (1943), p. 181. Robert McKay ("The Preference for Freedom," p. 1182) insists that only Frankfurter explicitly denied the preference notion.
25. *Craig* v. *Harney*, 331 U.S. 367 (1947), p. 391.

majority of the sitting Justices' acquiescence. Whereas at least six Justices indicated their acceptance of the doctrine as an approach,[26] their interpretations were highly diverse and often antagonistic.

Nor were the libertarians adept at providing a justification in history or law for their position—perhaps because they saw the need for greater protection as self-evident, but more probably because that precious judicial commodity, time, was denied them. Their day was brief indeed; only half a decade marked the efflorescence of this compelling shadow doctrine that knew no clearcut triumphs and disappeared without a defeat, almost without a confrontation, and yet most indelibly marked future litigation on the First Amendment.

Certainly, the "preference for freedom" is profoundly rooted in our history. The judicial traditions of at least four states explicitly provide the basis for such a differentiation of constitutional provisions;[27] so does a great deal of federal litigation in administrative law and elsewhere.[28] But the libertarians were unable to synthesize or even present these materials in any but the most piecemeal fashion. Ironically, it was Frankfurter who was to write the history of the doctrine as an overt approach. And Frankfurter was successful in his obvious effort to turn his historical treatment into an epitaph. Noting attribution of "preferred freedoms" origins to the Carolene Products footnote, he challenged the appropriateness of such a form for new doctrines. He denied that a majority had accepted such an approach—a statement that was technically true—and attacked the logic of its prem-

---

26. Samuel Krislov, "The Supreme Court Since 1937: Nine Judges in Search of a Role," (unpublished Ph.D. dissertation, Princeton University, 1955 [University microfilms]), p. 80.

27. Samuel Krislov, "Mr. Justice Black Reopens the Free Speech Debate," *UCLA Law Review,* XI (1964), 204–6.

28. McKay, "The Preference for Freedom," p. 1182. See, for an early presentation of this view W. D. L. Lewis, "The Proper Canon of Interpretation of Bills of Rights in a Written Constitution," *University of Pennsylvania Law Review,* XLI (1892), 782.

ises in strong terms; from that moment on, its disappearance was rapid, although no specific repudiation took place.

Even as a canon of construction, the "preferred freedoms" approach was faint-hearted. It seems more in the nature of a halfway house between the balancing of interests and the absolutist positions. Further, as a center of controversy in the late 1940s and early 1950s, the doctrine hardly seems worth the antagonism that its use created. In this respect, it rather resembles "clear and present danger" and "clear and probable danger," variations that have recently been ignored by the Justices as having been largely sapped of vitality although still arousing animosity.

It had, however, one great advantage; it reflected a state of mind representative of the attitudes of the Justices and a prevailing popular sentiment that favored expression but recognized the need for limitations. It is a weak, inexact, lawyerly instrument, rather less helpful than most in deciding a specific case, prescribing neither a method for decision nor guidance in determining the line between invalidation or acceptance. It has, however, within it a clear reminder to the judiciary of the central significance of free expression. It is the lack of such a reminder in both the balancing and clear and probable danger tests that accounts for their peculiar lack of appeal.

The relegation of the "preferred freedoms" doctrine to a kind of never-never land has left the field to the two dominant approaches—balancing and absolutism—whose dimensions suffer not only from inexactness, but also because their terms exaggerate doctrinal differences and differences in the practical ends sought by the opposing sets of judges. The reconciliation of these approaches in practical decision-making—or, more precisely, such degree of reconciliation as has occurred—has been achieved through the judicial backdoor by means of a series of secondary or auxiliary rules of decision that are more or less acceptable to and used by diverse members of the Court.

JUDICIAL STANDARDS: "CLEAR AND PRESENT DANGER"

The first and hardiest of the auxiliary standards is the "clear and present danger" test, which, as noted, has been soft-pedaled but never repudiated by the Justices over a period of two decades. Speaking of the "Hand–Vinson discount balance" technique in the Dennis Case, one observer notes that "this reinterpretation of the 'clear and present danger' test appears to have killed it" and that the Court "has never again expressly asked itself" Hand's question on justification for invasion of free speech.[29] Most authorities have assumed that it has been tacitly discarded, and *Shepard's Citations* tends to support this by listing no cases since Dennis under that heading. The best clue is probably Justice Brennan's comment on the relative scope of various tests. It would appear that the "clear and present danger" test has been confined to the type of case for which it was first developed: a crowd or similarly incendiary situation, as a boundary indicator between permissible expression and regulatable action. In Scales v. United States, Dennis was seemingly followed, although the Yates Case basically interred Dennis as a clear precedent. The Court, however, continues to use the same sort of reasoning—in the Holmes–Brandeis sense, without the Hand emendation—without discussion by label as "clear and present danger" in a number of cases such as Wood v. Georgia.[30]

Even in a more limited sense, the test does not seem likely to endure. It is not terribly appealing to an absolutist because it still focuses on the possibility of regulating expression prior to any overt act. Thus Roger Baldwin, the very personification of the American Civil Liberties Union, observed in 1936 "that with clear and present danger the

---

29. Laurent Frantz, "The First Amendment in the Balance," *Yale Law Journal*, LXXI (1962), 1428.
30. 370 U.S. 375 (1962). See also *Cox v. Louisiana*, 379 U.S. 476 (1965), pp. 565–6.

door was opened wide for legal suppression to enter. And it
has come in and made itself at home since."[31] Meiklejohn
wrote his little book largely in protest against "a peculiarly
inept and unsuccessful attempt to formulate an exception to
the principle of the freedom of speech."[32]

So absolutism emerged almost as a revolt against "clear
and present danger," and support, if any, must largely come
from the balancers. But, in truth, they too are largely dis-
enchanted, and their reaction to rules in this domain is quite
similarly a product of what they regard as an oversimplified
and premature attempt at generalized formulations. "Clear
and present danger" is, to be sure, essentially a balancing formula; but, to sophisticated balancers, it suggests a simplifica-
tion of the problem, an incomplete enumeration of the
factors involved in balancing.[33] This distortion is at a minimum in face-to-face situations. Yet, even there, external factors are not typically considered, and little play is given to a
relative evaluation of the significance of the speech or the
seriousness of the evil. In short, less freedom is given the
judge than the balancers prefer.

This, in turn, suggests the obvious: that, particularly in

---

31. Roger Baldwin, "Personal Liberty," *Annals,* CLXXXV (1936), 164.
32. Meiklejohn, *Political Freedom,* p. 45.
33. See, for example, Paul's Freund's influential and much-quoted suggestion
    that other matters be included: relative danger, value of the expres-
    sion, availability of alternative regulations, and perhaps motives, in
    The Supreme Court of the United States (New York: Meridian Books,
    1961), p. 44. The progressive disillusionment of the present balancers
    is well encapsulated in the evolution of views of Wallace Mendelson.
    In 1952, in "The Clear and Present Danger Test—A Reply to Mr.
    Meiklejohn," *Vanderbilt Law Review,* V (June, 1952), 792, Mendelson
    argued that Meiklejohn was unfair to Holmes. "Clear and present
    danger" was a constitutionally warranted doctrine that differentiated
    words and deeds, that is, a difference of kind, and did not balance
    speech against other interests. Within half a decade, Mendelson was
    to embrace the position he had previously implied was unconstitu-
    tional. That the effect of Dennis v. United States was to reduce "clear
    and present danger" to balancing was correctly understood by another
    constitutional authority writing at the very same time. See Edward
    S. Corwin, "Bowing Out 'Clear and Present Danger,'" *Notre Dame
    Lawyer,* XXVII (Spring, 1952), 326. Corwin also correctly anticipated
    virtually the precise limits to which future courts would use the "clear
    and present danger" approach.

face-to-face situations, the "clear and present danger" test, being relatively more ministerial in its application, is more acceptable than balancing to the absolutists. The test seems, therefore, not only especially suited to such problems, but also least objectionable, if not particularly attractive, to both sides. Its survival may thus be a product of a feeling that it is not worth the acrimony involved in repudiating it—at least in the absence of another, agreed-upon test. As it is, it has survived as a sort of buffer between the two major points of view, but one not likely to remain—if, indeed, it has not already disappeared.

APPLIED STANDARDS: "VOID ON ITS FACE"

In contrast, another technique, not quite so venerable but still of pre-Roosevelt Court vintage, has grown in its use in recent years and seems likely to wax as "clear and present danger" wanes. Declaring a statute "void on its face" was a technique perfected by no less a figure than Chief Justice Hughes in one of the cases considered to have re-established the "clear and present danger" rule.

The distinctiveness of this method of invalidating a statute is perhaps not immediately apparent. Normally, legislation is not challengeable in the Courts until implemented or applied. In general, a ruling on constitutionality is not given by the Supreme Court in abstract terms on the basis of merely potential loss or threat to a party. Such "advisory opinions" are in fact rendered by international courts, British courts, and, among others, the Massachusetts General Court. For the United States Supreme Court, however, a matter must be "ripe for review," and the threatened loss must have occurred and redress sought before the Court will entertain a plea for relief. (An extreme and often criticized example occurred when Immigration authorities ruled aliens going to Alaska would be treated on return as immigrants from abroad. Cannery workers who wished to work a summer in Alaska sought a Court injunction and were told the matter was not yet "ripe for review." Only if the workers ran the risk of perpetual expulsion from the United States would the courts deal with the matter.) Until administrators or judges construe a statute, it is not clear that issues of constitutionality would have to be faced, for an interpretation might be arrived at that satisfied the claim. The principles of "ripeness for review" and its cousin, "exhaustion of administrative and local remedies," suggest that a claim of unconstitutionality of a law will not be heard until construed by judges or appropriate administrators.

Hughes' sanction of treatment of statutes abridging basic freedoms in different fashion was, therefore, an innovation of no mean proportions. Essentially, he accepted the proposition that the mere risk of invasion of civil liberties was sufficiently threatening and inhibiting to free expression to justify a radical shift in the judicial role. Hughes' towering reputation as a judge and as a responsible conservative was, therefore, directly invoked in behalf of a position most compatible with the "preferred freedoms" and absolutist positions to be developed more than a decade later. Not as a zealot, but as a consistent craftsman with a libertarian point of view, Hughes perfected a tool that proved to have its greatest practical utility to a later bench of more libertarian hue—with the added benefit that the device was clearly of more respectable, older vintage.

This technique was, to a large extent, perfected and buttressed by Justice Roberts for a unanimous Court in the Cantwell Case. If a statute in the domain of free speech is overly broad, the Court can invalidate, even though a more narrowly drawn statute might have reached the conduct of the defendant involved in the case. Thus, the usual efforts of the Supreme Court to avoid issues of constitutionality are to be relaxed in the domain of expression.

Since "voiding on its face" permits decision before a "total" fact situation is fully developed, it requires judicial decision on a rule-making basis. It is, therefore, somewhat antithetical to ad hoc balancing, for some of the factual considerations are of necessity not yet developed. Additionally, the method is, to a large extent, an acceptance of the key protective concept of preferred freedoms and absolutism since it puts prevention of even possible threats to freedom in the forefront of the judge's responsibility.

It is, however, a technique rendered more compatible with traditional judicial responsibility not only by its comparatively long standing—as civil liberties techniques go, anyway—and its authoritative source, but also because of its analogy with the traditional equity relief that may be granted on a showing of irreparable damage. Given this reasonable affinity for both sides, "voiding on its face" can be expected to be used increasingly in a matter-of-fact manner and without elaborate justification of its ideological underpinnings— particularly if the present pattern of clear and libertarian plurality, with shifting majority lineups, persists.

The significance and utility of the doctrine has been amply demonstrated in the sit-in and other civil-rights demonstrations of recent years. Except for the possibility of acting on the basis of the wording of legislation, the courts might have been compelled to sit by as restrictive legislation, knowingly unconstitutional, was passed to prevent specific civil-rights efforts. After it had served its purpose, the legislation would then be interred by the courts in what would have been a most solemn farce. If the "void on its face" doctrine had not been available, it would have been necessary to invent it in recent years.

APPLIED STANDARDS: REASONABLE ALTERNATIVES

Yet another, perhaps more gradually and less clearly developed, standard has been the one summarized as the "doctrine of the reasonable alternative." In essence, it suggests that, if a regulatory scheme—say a licensing of parades to avoid traffic congestion—has the effect of retarding expression, the regulation may not be upheld if another method of achieving the government's purpose is available that would avoid repression. This is similar to another lawyerly proposition—that a statute must not be needlessly over-broad in its application. For example, our parade ordinance might require registration where twelve or more persons congregate in a public thoroughfare, but the judges would be at least dubious about the appropriateness of requiring a permit where two or more congregate. But the reasonable alternative goes further than a rational or due process test and seeks to protect rights from that infringement that is in practical terms not necessary. Although the doctrine of the reasonable alternative is logically and legally separable from "voiding on its face," it is closely related.

It is primarily the balancers who use this rather vaguely formed doctrine and, as discussed earlier, in somewhat inconsistent form. At times, the test requires that there be no reasonable alternative that will satisfy an overweening governmental interest; here, although there is some balancing, a very strong presumption in favor of the individual is operating. At other times, it is suggested, the alternatives must be closely matched in efficiency and coverage. In other words, it is not enough to show that the *primary* (or overweening) interest can be satisfied; secondary considerations may so balance the picture that the alternative may even be superior with regard to the central interest, and, yet, in applying this version of the test, the Court will not invalidate. The difference is between any alternative and one demonstrably superior in every respect, which is a difference indeed.

But it can be most favorable to free expression, when attempts are made to measure the marginal governmental interest in dealing with a subject. In this particular form, it narrows the balance struck—and in favor of the individual. He need not so much show that his interests outweigh all conceivable governmental concern with this subject, but only its concern expressed in this unique way, with all the weaknesses of the specified regulation. At its most favorable, then, the device clearly protects rights and virtually reverses the presumption of constitutionality by requiring a showing that there was no other way to achieve the governmental purpose. Therefore, it approaches the absolutist position, although it permits consideration of governmental needs.[34] Since it can be presented as a technical decision rule rather than as a doctrine of constitutional interpretation, it arouses less animosity and quietly reduces the difference between wings of the Court. It may well be found increasingly appealing as time passes.

STANDARDS UNSTANDARDIZED BUT EFFICACIOUS

Many of the subsidiary devices used by the Court, it would appear, are added weights normally tossed on the side of disputed rights or freedoms. It becomes of little practical moment what image of judging one uses if one insists on more stringent rules of governmental justification and develops more lenient rules for judicial intervention. The difference tends to become a verbal one most of the time, with practical outcomes generally the same and with a consequent narrowing of the controversy to highly specific issues. This is a process that has already been evident in such matters as interstate taxation. Convergence is a development that theoretically should occur through time in the judicial process and in pressure-cooker, hurry-up fashion in a colleaguial Court. There is some evidence that this is in fact what is happening with regard to Supreme Court attitudes toward civil liberties as trial and error and basic success to

---

34. See Wormuth and Mirkin, "The Doctrine of the Reasonable Alternative," for a thoughtful discussion.

date seem to prick out lines of Court strategy for the future.

Although the particular issues that precipitated the present cleavage on the Court no longer loom as large as a decade ago, they are central ones. The relationship of the judiciary to the legislature and the public, the obligation to a tradition of freedom, and the constitutional obligation imposed by the very exercise of judicial review are seminal questions that previous Justices did not have to—or occasionally refused to—face up to. The Stone, Vinson, and Warren Courts have contributed in a major way to delineating these problems and amassing powerful arguments on various sides of complex issues.

This basic tribute having been made, more grudging and critical comment must be added. It seems unlikely that the grand approaches over which most of the controversy has taken place are likely to be accepted in toto, and it is doubtful that either absolutism or balancing will be enshrined in decisions by 1970. They were both too much the products of a single era, too precisely framed, to cope with the issues of popular response to the threat of international Communism, too much the product of dialectical disagreement between their leading protagonists to be easily adaptable to long-term needs.

Already, balancing has been demonstrated to be too amorphous a doctrine to require even the courtesy of repudiation, too vague an admonition to channel decisions; the doctrine lacks the fundamental requirement of reminding the Justices of the special requirements for protection of the political process and of distinguishing, even in a general way, between the occasions for Court abnegation and those of Court intervention. Indeed, the paradox of balancing is that it demands great involvement from the judge in the immediate result of the decision, although the balancers generally claim to be "judicial-minded" and act in the name of restraint. That confusion of roles in itself indicates real problems with the presently debated positions, suggesting that some profound semantic confusion—perhaps in both camps—has resulted from the particular set of circumstances and personalities distilled under the two labels. The balancers are almost to a man Frankfurterites who argue for neutral general principles, but who insist that judges take into account circumstances of time and place—including public and legislative reaction to decisions—that are the quintessence of expediency rather than broad doctrine. The result, Gerald Gunther has suggested in a brilliant and careful study of the approach of Alexander Bickel, a leading spokesman for balancing and restraint, is "100% insistence on principle, 20% of the time."[35]

But absolutism seems a poorly articulated notion, a mysterious gambit, even after a decade of judicial exposure. If the peculiar weakness of its chief rivals is their lack of psychological signaling of the need for protection of expression, the peculiar weakness of absolutism is its paralyzing effect on thought itself—not just judicial thought, but also that of the general public. It promises something it cannot deliver in an ordered society—untrammeled discussion unfettered by time and circumstances. It encourages naïveté, and it betokens disillusionment when more realistic standards come into play. The public surprise—shock would not be too strong a word —at some of Justice Black's quite consistent civil-rights demonstration decisions illustrates the point. Furthermore, little is gained by controlling the judges—presumably one of Black's major quests—for, in determining what is direct regulation of content and what is merely regulation of circumstances, semantic ambiguities give quite enough leeway to make who is judging more significant than the test used. It is likely that insistence on a differentiation between ideas and actions—with all of the difficulties that will be discussed in the next chapter—will achieve the same positive results with less camouflage of issues. It is confusing, after all, to

35. Gerald Gunther, "The Subtle Vices of the 'Passive Virtues,'" *Columbia Law Review*, LXIV (1964), 3.

have absolutists vote against a freedom defended by tenta-
tivists.

During the past era seminal issues and architectonic solutions were emphasized—"a general theory of the First Amendment" and an absolute answer (framed by a philosopher
basically in the pragmatic tradition!). Perhaps it will be
regarded as a sign of failure, perhaps a tribute to the Justices'
aspirations, or perhaps merely another indictment of the
human condition that the questions raised during the past
two decades loom as more satisfactory than the solutions.

4

Issues and Dilemmas

So far we have proceeded like the man crossing the room in one of Zeno's famous paradoxes; with each chapter, we have moved down the ladder of abstraction and statements of ideological approaches to free speech, but we still have fallen short of dealing with concrete problems. In this chapter, we shall deal with what has traditionally been regarded as concrete problems and their resolution by Supreme Court fiat. As we shall see, even this level does not truly bring us face-to-face with everyday effects of decisions. They are implemented not by judges, but by administrators and policemen whose approach to problems, whose mode of thought, is different from and even antithetical to legal processes. Only in the legal or formal sense, then, have we completed our quest for the concrete, the "lawstuff," the units

of human behavior that constitute the source and end of
regulatory activity.

Why should such regulation present problems in a
society that has clearly accepted the value of free expression as paramount and central to its operations? But that
agreement is delusive and in fact is distinguished by its
absence. "All declare for 'liberty,'" wrote Justice Reed,
"and proceed to disagree among themselves as to its true
meaning."[1]

As even the absolutist Meiklejohn notes, no society can
permit the right of expression to override all regulation
everywhere. The town meeting, he observed, can be ad-
journed if the building is collapsing or, say, an epidemic is
threatened. Similarly, Justice Black admits—even proclaims
—in causes involving civil-rights demonstrations, "the Constitution . . . does not take away the state's power, indeed its
duty, to keep order and do justice. . . ."[2] Thus, even absolutists admit the relevance of other rights and the interests
of other claimants to rights in determining the extent of the
privileges of the claimant before the Court. It is the limits
imposed by nature, man, and social life that compel an
examination of rights to consider other claims. The ambiguity of decision and the disagreement in specific instances
results from different ways of weighing in different claims.

Efforts to resolve conflicts of interests by simplistic
formulae or automatic equations produce the same diversity
of answers that discrete individuals with contradictory value
systems produce. Thus, the standard formula that "your right
to swing your arm ends where my nose begins" had been seen
by some, like the fear of the Lord, as the beginning of wisdom. But, in fact, the epigram produces virtually no guidance
at all. There are times when one should avoid thrusting a
nose in front of a fist and other occasions—say with a burglar
entering your premises—when you may lay it on with relative impunity. Once realistic conflicts are admitted as pos-

---

1. *Breard* v. *Alexandria,* 341 U.S. 622 (1951), p. 625.
2. *Cox* v. *Louisiana,* 379 U.S. 536, 559 (1965), p. 584.

sible, contradictory evaluation with regard to relative importance of the competing values is inevitable.

The effort to translate Mill's approach—or the more general utilitarian calculus—into a decision-making scheme with regard to even less emotion-ridden issues has reached an impasse. Even in balancing such matters as the financial success of a business—say a paint factory—with risk of skin disease, it is impossible to balance units of gain and loss. (How many bankruptcies should equal or outweigh a hundred cases of mild impetigo?) Only essentially arbitrary decisions or conventional practices break the logical impasse. Where issues involve self-identity and the emotional problems attending self-expression and its denial, the lack of convincing impersonal standards is even more apparent.

As soon as one admits some limitations on individual enterprise, some control must be imposed. It is not merely the concessions of Black and Meiklejohn that cause the dilemma, but rather the clear necessities of the case. The simple inability of two men to occupy the same space at the same time compels either social regulation or a society that so completely internalizes cooperative values that no conflict will result. But the latter alternative itself requires comprehensive socialization of a type creating a different and deeper conflict of values. Such a program of education necessarily involves the government in spheres of activity commonly thought of as private. Even in a society that prides itself on the limited scope of government, the domain of private activity is constantly an issue.

Far from simple resolution, the line between freedom and authority is an indistinct, wavering one, subject to constant re-evaluation. These two social needs have historically emerged as antinomies and, as John Stuart Mill informs us, "the balance hit upon by each generation has never failed to dismay the next."[3] Niebuhr has suggested that "man's capacity for justice makes democracy possible, but man's incli-

3. John Stuart Mill, *On Liberty* (London: Oxford University Press, 1948), p. 10.

nation to injustice makes democracy necessary."[4] Only a slight paraphrase is necessary to suggest that it is the aspirations of man that make free expression necessary and that his limitations compel its regulation.

THE LIMITATIONS OF TIME AND SPACE

The mental image of free speech that libertarians conjure up is of an idealized "Hyde Park" situation, with small, rapt groups gathered around various speakers of all hues. It is the libertarian equivalent, perhaps, of Adam Smith's marketplace—and, probably, an even less realistic model. Hyde Park is one small area in a sprawling metropolis, whereas the principles deduced from its example would extend the same rights almost indefinitely. But the image of a society completely engrossed in or, at least, dedicated to furious discussion is not only not a picture of a happy society; it is not even the portrait of a viable society. "In the beginning was the word" does not justify a society totally devoted to the word. Assuredly man cannot live by bread alone, but, as Jane Eyre pointed out, it is most difficult to live without it. Greek society, with its slave base, could in some ways approximate a debating fraternity, but only for a small segment of the population. Safety regulations, normal traffic flow, some method for controlling speakers who simultaneously seek to speak, and control of the heckler must admittedly be served through regulation. If anyone has the power to suspend all aspects of social life at his whim, his rights are enhanced, but it is doubtful that such a state of affairs would represent maximization of liberty for the society as a whole. The rest of society would be reduced to a captive audience; we would become a generalized case of the Lar Daly problem. (Daly, a perennial candidate for public office whose distinctiveness

---

4.   Reinhold Niebuhr, *The Children of Light and the Children of Darkness*, (New York: Chas. Scribner's Sons, 1944), p. xi.

seems to lie exclusively in his campaign custom—an Uncle Sam suit—has demanded, at first successfully, equal use of scarce radio and television time with his "opponents" for such office as President. The effect was to prevent granting time to any candidate or to devote scarce television and radio time to any and all candidates, many of them irrelevant or inconsequential.) Social channels of communication are perhaps more restricted than television channels; yet, any grant of autonomous definition of time, manner, and place of expression threatens to become a serious denial to others of their own purposes and human needs. A loudspeaker in the middle of the night is a hindrance to sleep that can be prevented without profound philosophical justification.

But the problem that arises from granting the right to regulate also ensues from human frailty and is ageless—who guards the guardians? The power to decide the reasonableness of the circumstances in which free expression may take place is not identical with but easily becomes the power to fix the content of expression. On this thin line between regulation and control lies the essence of free government.

The general principles seem clear, but the application is subtle and elusive. Governments may reasonably regulate the time and manner of the use of public facilities. These regulations however must be generally precise and must permit a minimum of discretion on the part of licensing or other public officials. Regulations should not be so framed as to eliminate a mode of discourse that is unique to or more favored by some potential interest. (Handbills specifically may not be prohibited even as a sanitation regulation, the Supreme Court has decided, since they constitute a favorite mode of expression for groups for whom it is hard to find an alternative method at so reasonable a cost.[5]) Permits and

5. *Lovell* v. *Griffin*, 303 U.S. 444 (1938); in *Talley* v. *California*, 362 U.S. 60 (1960), the Court went further, invalidating a Los Angeles requirement that handbills must have the name of the printer and distributor printed on them.

reasonable fees are not excluded so long as they are equitably enforced, and traffic, fire, and other safety measures may properly be enforced. In the Feiner Case, as noted, the hidden dangers in these innocuous statements became apparent. To a callow soapbox orator capable of such profundities as "Mayor Costello is a champagne-sipping bum," his audiences' interference with traffic is likely to appear nil. To a policeman intent on avoiding trouble, the audience may become an obstruction if one person's left heel hangs over a curb. The policeman's "menace from the crowd" is the speaker's "pleasant heckler" adding interest to the discussion. Discretion in the policeman, checked by a jealous legal system and zealous citizens—including a network of civil-rights organizations—has so far been the only, and partial, answer to the problem of drawing the line.

In the public street, rights of expression collide mainly with the needs of traffic and safety. In the absence of such considerations, the right of passage and even assembly should prevail. In various civil-rights cases, this was firmly asserted, as, for example, in the reversal of convictions of demonstrators for questioning a policeman's right to summarily end a public meeting without explanation or for violating vague prohibitions of disorderly conduct or loitering. Thus Negroes and white sympathizers could assemble near a city hall in effect to petition for the right to register as long as they were peaceable and did not unreasonably restrict access to the building or to the flow of traffic. Even a widespread march on the highways was permitted by Federal Judge Frank Johnson in Alabama, reasoning that the redress sought required some massive manifestation.[6] Similarly, parks are appropriate for meeting as long as they are not destructive of other purposes.[7]

But what of other public facilities such as swimming pools, schools, and libraries? Each can be used for public

6. *Time,* May 12, 1967.
7. *Hague* v. *CIO* (1937).

expression, although normally there are competing, more standard, uses. The clearest principle is that, if the governmental unit chooses to open such facilities as forums, it must do so equitably. Thus Hunter College, operated by the Board of Higher Education of the City of New York, which regularly rented its auditorium to various public groups, was legally required to offer its facilities at regular rentals to William Buckley and the *National Review,* although some of the college's officials and faculty did not take kindly to conservative views.[8]

But what if there has been no dedication of the public facility to purposes of discussion? Barring a total absence of other facilities, which would raise some novel problems, it does not appear that one could compel such usage. Citizens who wished to demonstrate or otherwise use the public facility would then seem to come under the principles implicit in the Library Sit-in Case. There, convictions of demonstrators who stood quietly in a public library were dismissed. Apparently, the Court proceeded on the theory, that as long as their conduct was within the normal bounds accorded to regular users, they were not in violation. If they had attempted to stay beyond the intervals accorded readers or in some way had actively interfered with library process, they could have been excluded or punished. These general, largely common-sense tests would seem widely applicable to public properties other than libraries as well.

But Brown *v.* Louisiana, the case in point, was only a 5–4 decision, with Justice Black writing a dissent on the grounds, apparently, that a public library was simply an improper place for protest—even if the protest was of the

---

8. *Buckley* v. *Meng,* 230 N.Y.S. 2d, 924 (1962). In *Egan* v. *Moore,* 245 N.Y.S. 2d, 622 (1963), analogous reasoning was used to rule that public universities may not arbitrarily restrict speakers on campuses. California state and municipal laws requiring those wishing to rent public halls to file loyalty oaths were invalidated, but an ordinance requiring an affirmation that the user did not intend to knowingly use the premises for any illegal purpose was upheld.

library's segregation policies. (In my judgment, Justice
Black's dissent in this case is peculiar and unjustifiable by
normal standards. Perhaps the clue is in his stated fears that
the Court opinion would be understood as sanctioning an
unlimited right of demonstration.)

This general issue has produced three other decisions by
this narrowest of margins—and on opposite sides of the question. In both instances, however, majority and dissenters
focused on the specific fact situations to such an extent as
to narrow the differences between the two wings much more
than would appear at first glance. Earlier, in Cox *v.* Louisiana, the Court had set aside conviction of civil-rights demonstrators who had massed in front of a courthouse and had
been found guilty on various grounds including an intent to
obstruct justice. Conceding the right of a state to prevent
court room intimidation, the Court held that the suggestion
of officials that the group assemble across the street was a
waiver or perhaps an interpretation of the statute. The law
was valid, but, in the full set of circumstances, no violation
had occurred. The dissenters did not find this plausible,
either on the facts or as a matter of law. In the Adderley
Case, the roles were reversed. The new majority found it
improper for demonstrations to be held on jailhouse grounds
after official warning. Justice Black emphasized the indications in the record that no similar demonstrations had ever
been permitted and that impediment to traffic had resulted
from massing on the grounds. The dissenters found fault in
the generality of the statute, which gave discretionary power
to the officials; had there been a clear statutory restriction
or a sign posted in advance, they, too, would apparently have
acquiesced. In Walker *v.* Alabama this same majority indicated demonstrators had no right to challenge a questionable
injunction by going out into the streets.

It would appear, then, that a state may curtail use of its
premises to expression when that usage is inimical to the
purpose of the facility. The disagreement seems to focus on

the degree of discretion to be accorded individual officers, although clearly discriminatory application is forbidden. Furthermore, governments may act to protect property rights of citizens. For example, it may prevent a group from taking over a hall without payment of the standard rental without creating a free-speech issue. But the line between government stepping in to protect property rights and acting on its own to effectuate a denial of liberty of expression is a most subtle one. Even before the civil-rights demonstrations forced the issue, it was clear that suppression could be defended in the name of property and that extreme care had to be exercised in scrutinizing legislation of this sort. Thus, an ordinance requiring permission of householders prior to ringing doorbells was invalidated for individuals going door to door to disseminate religious ideas, although a similar ordinance was sustainable for peddlers or merchants.[9] The civil-rights demonstrations also clarified some issues (although, as we shall see, they obfuscated others) by suggesting that, when government sets in motion a policy that might well coerce individual property owners to in turn invoke the machinery of government, state action is involved that must meet the standards of the Fourteenth Amendment. If, as for example occurred in the Lombard Case, a mayor or police chief announces in advance, "We will not tolerate these demonstrations," quite different constitutional standards prevail than when an individual property owner calls up to complain unexpectedly, "Some nuts are overrunning my property." In the first instance, government is acting as judge of the effort at expression, and it must meet the full standards of the Fourteenth Amendment, that is, the situation must be one that it could regulate under First Amendment standards. In the second instance, even legitimate unsuppressible opinion may be forced into proper channels without involving the question of governmental control over content.

---

9. *Martin* v. *Struthers* 319 U.S. 141 (1943).

But in any event, where no other avenue for free expression exists, previous bets are off. In a company town, where the very avenues are the property of someone and where the sole auditorium belongs to private enterprise, the reality that the company is the government will prevail. Like a government, it must make facilities dedicated to public use available in nondiscriminatory fashion; like a government, it can reasonably channel but cannot cut off the flow of ideas.[10]

COMPETING VALUES: CONTENT OF SPEECH AND ITS REGULATION

As difficult as the problem of circumstances of speech is, it must fade before the more vexatious question of regulation of content. To be sure, our society contends that it does not so regulate speech. Yet, only highly artificial distinctions separate individual threats—"Someday I'll kill you"—from some ideological programs—"All people in mental institutions for more than a decade should be gassed." For legal purposes, we distinguish between ideas and words that are entrained actions, that carry with them consequences of deeds. In so doing, we quite properly take into account those words that are the triggers to action, evaluate their consequences, and occasionally regulate them. But all too often, the test we must apply to determine whether they constitute deeds are the effects on others or the motives of the speaker, rather than some actual action on his part.

Until recently, the most clearcut and unexceptionable example that could be cited of this would have been libel and slander laws. Even now, the defection of Mr. Justice Black does not make a winter; and it is clear that the bulk of such laws constitute a limitation on untrammeled self-

---

10. *Marsh* v. *Alabama* 326 U.S. 501 (1946).

expression. Although an occasional individual may engage in a serious, systematic effort to ruin another person through libel or slander—that is, he is consciously engaged in a deed the dimensions of which are known to him—the fact is that the bulk of such cases have a stray, inadvertent, aleatory, and even arbitrary element to them. Libel and slander tend to sneak up on perpetrator and victim alike without much advance notice. What is technically speaking actionable and under what circumstances specific defenses are likely to prevail is a field of learning not too well mastered by nonspecialist lawyers, let alone laymen. It is the consequence of the words—all too often fictional or dubious legal consequences —or the vagaries of the jury, rather than any action by the defendant, that determines the punishment. (Even dictating a letter to a stenographer constitutes publication and exposes one to the severe standards of libel, while in most jurisdictions a statement in a television show remains merely slander, unless the program is taped or the remark read from a script.) We have noted the important departure made in the *New York Times* Case, which eliminates libel law in relation to public officers except under circumstances that should prove rather rare, and the subsequent effort to expand the concept to those who choose to occupy the public spotlight, the center of political controversy. The final rulings, however, are likely to leave unchanged the concept that private citizens far removed from public discussion can vindicate their reputations by collecting damages from other private citizens who make legally improper remarks—in spite of the limitation on expression entailed. Already the decision in Curtis Publishing *v.* Butts has insisted upon more usual standards of "due care" even when dealing with one technically a public official.

Libel is but one area where we are concerned with effects on the listener. Another prominent and historically related example is obscenity. In the final analysis, obscenity is apparently forbidden because of the sense of shock it creates in its beholders. Nudity, public fornication, and pornography are outlawed also in fear of supposed corruption of the youth by exposure to depravity; however, even hoary oldsters are protected by the reach of our laws.

Of the two claims, indeed, the impressionability of youth is perhaps the most exaggerated. Evidence would suggest that parents generally control the values of their children and that where they do not, it is the "push" of rejection of the home rather than the "pull," the attraction of Sodom and Gomorrah, that is the causal force. Chesterton, whose strongly religious commitment did not blind him to the realities of psychological influence, is brilliant on this point. Noting that a child was supposed to have killed his father with a carving knife as a result of seeing such an episode in a movie, he observed:

> This may possibly have occurred. . . . But what is supposed to be the practical moral of it, in any case? Is it that the young should never see a story with a knife in it? . . . It would be more practical that a child should never see a real carving knife and still more practical that he should never see a real father. . . . If the cinema exhibited nothing but views of country vicarages or vegetarian restaurants the ugly fancy is as likely to be stimulated by these.[11]

It is more likely that what is at stake is more the parental desire to monopolize at least in part the environment of the young child than a threat to the morality of the minor exposed to such matters, and perhaps that claim has merit in the light of reciprocal parental obligations. On the other hand, pornography can be experienced as an affront, a blow, a shock, and it is mainly on this basis that it is regulated. (I myself once found a young coed incoherent and in tears after witnessing a campus exhibitionist who exposed himself in front of an inside window while hiding his face behind a

---

11. Quoted in Walter Gellhorn, *Individual Freedom and Governmental Restraints* (Baton Rouge: Louisiana State Press, 1956), p. 65.

rolled up window shade. The experience was so ugly it took several minutes for her even to regain enough composure to tell us what happened so that we could call the campus police. Similar incidents recur.) But, given the wide variety of human tastes, it is clear that not every objection to every sort of conduct can be honored. Rather, the standard of prevailing community sentiment was long used, rejecting the use of more limited audiences, such as juveniles, as the litmus group. In recent years, the development of sharp differences in social attitudes on such matters became even more apparent than in the past. The concept of community standards became increasingly inadequate. Even the prohibition of hard core pornography—presumably that which anyone would acknowledge to be pornography—did not prove adequate on application to specific instances; clearly, pornographic effects are, in fact, used by some artists for motives that are perhaps only revealed by the work as a whole—and then only if the artist is successful in his execution.[12] The Court, therefore, has been reaching for more complex formulations, recognizing the sentiment for broader latitude and balancing the elements of the work in question, and, after experimenting with the rather unworkable game of deducing purpose from execution, it has settled on the more objective deduction from mode of distribution. The argument is sometimes advanced that this will lead to a situation where the most conservative advertising will in fact become the sign of outrageous obscenity in a work. But, if so, it would appear that it will be those sensitive to the little nuances of such perverse forms of promotion who will find their way—and would have anyway—whereas those not interested will hopefully be spared the nuisance of oh-so-artful mailings and screaming advertisements.

It is also argued persuasively that such titillation is not unique to advertising books, that the suave *New Yorker* ads

---

12. See the review of *The Story of O* in the *New York Times Book Review*, March 2, 1966.

for luxurious cars and the tawdry hard-sell commercial for a half-dollar deodorant are created to share the implied promise of an ultimately sexual benefit—the final vindication of mass democracy. But this is a curiously naïve argument that refuses to acknowledge the two-step nature of the inquiry; basically, the product must be evaluated as pornographic over and above the advertisement. It is the consumer object, not the lure, that is ultimately at stake. What is really being argued is that the panderer is no more morally reprehensible, since pandering is the Madison Avenue way of life. It is enough to note that this is a political argument, which might well be addressed to the legislature but does not really put advertising per se on all fours with an alleged pornographic work.

We can go farther. Critics of the Ginzburg decision are often those who believe in no moral censorship at all. It is doubtful that the majority of the population would really appreciate such a situation and even more doubtful—to me at least—that the issue is one of sufficient importance to really take great risks for it. In the meantime, while a national consensus develops, the Court has a test that adequately points out the most controversial questions without requiring exhausting, serial, and intense readings by the Justices. Nonetheless, as is made clear in a remarkable *per curiam* decision in Redrup *v.* New York, the Justices themselves remain badly divided on this issue.

In recent years, even libel and obscenity as distortions of free speech have been dramatically overshadowed by a third perplexing area, the domain of media handling of crime news. Here, where the stakes are so high for the accused, little if any protection is available beyond the threat of possible libel suits if acquittal occurs. Since solid experience demonstrates that sensational handling of crime stories, particularly murder coverage, sells newspapers, there is a great temptation in such events, which, on the whole, American journalism has succumbed to with gay abandon. The horrible example of the conduct of *The Cleveland Press* in the Sheppard murder trials is extreme, but it is only a composite and an exaggeration of typical newspaper behavior, creating a problem of considerable concern to all interested in making trials something more than an empty ritual.[13] The *Press* not only published daily front-page editorials proclaiming Sheppard's guilt and demanding his arrest and trial well before the authorities had reached their own conclusions, but also it maintained this tone of absolute certainty of guilt and implication of unworthiness of anyone with doubts in its coverage during the trial. It also continuously announced in its news columns, both before and during the proceedings, that damaging evidence and witnesses would be forthcoming that were in fact not later introduced in court. Since the newspaper was available to the jurors, the effect was to put in their minds evidence never in the record. Since such hysterical coverage usually generates its own wider audience, it would probably not have helped Sheppard nor any similar defendant to have received a change of venue.

The traditional solution has been for a judge to control excesses of media coverage through his power to punish for contempt of court. Such actions are summary proceedings in which the magistrate is indeed "judge and jury" and have therefore been viewed as a tainted means of enforcing equity. The judge in such situations could clearly do what Congress was apparently forbidden to do—interfere with freedom of the press. Not too surprisingly, perhaps, it would appear that judges are more sensitive to criticism of their own conduct than to other aspects of coverage. By single-handed, nontrial, sometimes secret proceedings judges could quell criticism of themselves through fine or imprisonment.

Led by Mr. Justice Black, the Supreme Court has, since the 1940s curtailed such uses of the contempt power, limit-

---

13. *Sheppard* v. *Maxwell*, 384 U.S. 333 (1966). Mr. Justice Black dissented without opinion. See also *Irvin* v. *Dowd*, 366 U.S. 717 (1961), which established the principle.

ing it in effect to events immediately arising in and around
the courtroom or necessarily affecting the proceedings. This
has, in turn, limited judicial power in controlling run-away
coverage by the press. To a certain extent, the Justices in
the Sheppard Case were rebuking Judge Blythin for not
doing things their decisions had previously suggested he
couldn't do; however, the Court made clear that "the carni-
val atmosphere of the trial itself was also improper," and
pointed to practices (such as permitting newspapermen to
handle evidence) that labeled his conduct as lax by any
standards.

Without strengthening the hand of trial judges to any
appreciable degree, however, the Supreme Court called on
them in the Sheppard Case to assert stricter control over
proceedings and coverage. Clearly as a consequence, judges'
conferences and a joint judicial–Bar Association Commission
late in 1966 called for development of a stricter code of newspaper coverage; they especially urged limiting police comment to bare-bones reporting of a crime and arrest and preventing such public disclosures as previous arrest record and
the evidence on which the trial would presumably proceed.
Whether such a code will be implemented, in what form,
and with what compliance by the press seems as difficult to
predict as the probability of its being challenged—and the
expectation of success of such challenge—on constitutional
grounds.

There has, however, been noticeable improvement—
with considerable room for future development—in coverage in such cases as the Speck murder trial. Comparatively
little incendiary material was released by the authorities; in
fact, a county psychiatrist was fired for revealing after the
trial (among other things) that Speck had virtually confessed
his guilt. A change of venue was permitted, the names of the
veniremen kept secret prior to the trial, the jury properly
sequestered, and the newsmen kept under considerable restraint—at least by Sheppard standards.

THE COMPETING VALUE
OF LAW AND ORDER

In the fullest sense, all of the offsetting claims to untrammelled expression discussed in this chaper are competing values; but none is as compelling as that based on the need for preserving the basic matrix of free expression, the forum for individual opinion—the society itself. We have already seen that such claims have been pressed in the judicial sphere and that fears for societal survival have found their expression in such decisions as Gitlow *v.* New York ("bad tendency" decision) and Dennis *v.* United States (the "clear and probable danger" standard).

It is sometimes asserted or implied in libertarian cant that societies face no danger from free expression—the societal analogue of "sticks and stones can break my bones but names will never hurt me." Even recent history fails to confirm this. The Nazis, for example, made great and effective use of all vehicles of communication, including political trials at which they exhorted, proclaimed, bullied, and challenged; they perfected the use of exhortation that implied threat and struck terror in their opponents. There is little in orthodox liberal notions about society as a polite center for exchange of ideas that would help cope with such challenges as these. To be sure, it is necessarily true that the Weimar Republic did not collapse solely because of the license accorded extremist groups; yet, it is difficult to believe that such deliberately destructive invective did not generate counterinvective to the detriment of any atmosphere of tranquility and civility necessary to effectively operate democratic government. The very machinery of such a government depends on self-restraint among the participants and limitation on types of discourse and action requiring both discipline and trust. (Giving up the right to eliminate opponents permanently is humanly likely only if there is some feeling that the action would be reciprocal if the situation were reversed.) The usual image of expression as a safety valve in a pressure cooker has some application, but, at times, expression rather is contained and in accordance with Pascal's law; pressure is transmitted undiminished in all directions. Circumstances control which image applies.

Yet, it must be acknowledged that the history of man suggests that governments are more apt to overreact to discussion than to permit an overabundance of it. And the machinery of incarceration and penalty is a crude and cumbersome mechanism more apt to create excess than to instill the sense of restraint through whole-hearted participation, postulated as the democratic ideal. Control of opinion is a harsh medicine, and the body politic should be ill indeed to use it at all:

> That community is already in the process of dissolution where each man begins to eye his neighbor as a possible enemy . . . where orthodoxy chokes freedom of dissent; where faith in the eventual supremacy of reason has become so timid we dare not enter our convictions in the open lists. . . .[14]

Thus, although a strong, even convincing theoretical argument can be assembled for suppression of those unwilling to abide by the rules of democracy (see chap. 1), experience suggests that such tampering is a cure literally more dangerous than the disease. We literally tolerate such expression not because of the moral position of its expounders, but because of the dictates of our own philosophy and the protection of our own rights.

Apparently, it has been universally considered that a state of war justifies the end of toleration. Quisling groups have been suppressed in even the most latitudinarian society. In our own, too, opposition to a war has generally been treated as criminal; in this century, however, much wider

---

14. Learned Hand, *The Spirit of Liberty,* p. 284 (from a speech given October 24, 1952).

accommodation of dissent has been accorded in each successive conflict. Indeed, the opposition to the Viet Nam effort has been accorded great scope, and the right to disagree has been defended vigorously and rather continuously by administrative spokesmen, from the President and Secretary of Defense on down. It is constitutionally and politically fortunate that they took this vigorous position, for technically, of course, no declaration of war was made in Viet Nam. If the precedent of possible suppression of free speech on the basis of unilateral presidential action were countenanced, a truly giant step toward an "age of Caesars" would have taken place in America.

For this reason, Mr. Richard Nixon's volunteered remarks on the Genovese Case—where a New Jersey professor had made pro-Viet Cong statements and a Republican candidate for Governor had called for his dismissal from the state university—in defense of suppression seem unfortunate and short-sighted:

> No one has questioned the right of Professor Genovese or anyone else to advocate any controversial issue in peacetime. . . .
>
> * * *
>
> I say as long as the demonstrators and those participating in teach-ins are acting in an individual and private capacity no action should be taken to curtail their activities.
>
> But any individual employed by the state should not be allowed to use his position for the purpose of giving aid and comfort to the enemies of the state.
>
> Where the choice confronting us is between the lives of American men fighting to preserve the system which guarantees freedom of speech for all and the right of an individual to abuse that freedom the lives of American fighting men must come first.[15]

In the Steel Seizure Case, the Supreme Court rejected the idea that a President could gain the right to seize property in

---

15. Letter to the editor, *New York Times,* October 29, 1965.

the United States through his military commitment of troops abroad; our rights of free speech should be even less subject to one individual's control.

Other voices have occasionally been heard to similar effect. Thus, for example, in May, 1967, members of the House armed Services Committee pressed for prosecution of draft foes during the testimony of Assistant Attorney General Vinson. Congressman Herbert of Louisiana asked first whether a law could be passed to "get around the First Amendment." When assured it did not seem possible, he suggested prosecution anyway: "Let's forget the First Amendment"; no member of the Committee verbally supported Vinson's defense of constitutional criteria.[16]

But official actions have been restrained and supportive of civil liberties. Thus, the Army court martial of Captain Howard Levy took seriously perhaps for the first time in history the legal question of right of dissent even within the ranks of the armed forces. This issue unresolved even in principle is not a frivolous one in an era of large, standing conscript armies. Court have held that conscription may not be used as a punishment for espousal of opposition to the war effort or any other official policy. But, if widespread conscription is accompanied by blanket requirements of conformity of expression, the habit of obedience will become that much more ingrained. On the other hand, armies usually have not been regarded as laboratories for majoritarian participation, and the vital power of authority must be assumed or the armed forces dissolved; if there is a need for standing armies, it is a need for effective *military* forces.

The Courts have also treated seriously, and by and large rejected, claims that such actions as burning draft cards are exempt from punishment on the grounds that it constitutes "symbolic speech." This rejection seems well-founded; all acts may have this symbolic sense to their perpetrators—

---

16. *New York Times,* May 6, 1967.

political assassination may well represent the epitome of symbolism; we forbid paramilitary uniforms and disguises (Ku Klux Klanners in robes) precisely because they symbolize—and therefore threaten and intimidate—exemption from law and order. The government often prescribes penalties for destruction and mutilation of official records or documents, and the principle should cover the draft-card burning issue. The one disturbing element is that the severity of the punishment is out of line with what is involved. (A $10 fine or so would seem more appropriate than the prescribed punishment—imprisonment.) Thomas Emerson has argued that the intent of Congress to suppress dissent as indicated by this penalty and the debate at the time of its adoption brings it under First Amendment prohibitions. This is an arguable position, but one that seems more compatible with legal norms and the realities of social life than the "symbolic speech" notion. Similarly and more emphatically, in the Julian Bond Case, the Justices found expression of dissent to our policy an insufficient basis for denial of a legislative seat. To reach this decision, the Court had to sweep aside the last vestiges of the "political questions" doctrine as it related to state agencies. In short, the Viet Nam crisis seems to be establishing guidelines for protection of liberty in cold-war situations.

But, in wartime, the immense power for repression in our constitutional system is untapped and undefined. We have had relatively little need to control groups dissenting from a war effort, although prosecutions in Warld War I of such groups became the major source of definition of freedom of speech. In World War II, a more circumspect leadership seldom sought court convictions but largely used administrative arrangements and voluntary cooperation with individuals and the mass media to secure their purposes, always holding in reserve the threat of more coercive measures. As the Japanese exclusion from California showed—albeit later confirmed by legislative action—the war powers of the President alone can drastically, almost totally, affect the liberties of vast portions of our citizenry; courts are not likely to challenge such exercise of power so long as military crisis prevails. As the focus of warfare becomes ever more diffuse, its effects will be ever more far-reaching. Although exact forms can hardly be imagined, drastic alterations in homefront liberties can nonetheless be anticipated in case of all-out war. If the prospect of modern warfare were not itself so benumbing, the probability of internal dislocation would loom as a major deterrent.

In any event, war is only the most threatening challenge to the normal operations of democracy and is well understood as an exceptional period, a highly temporary aberration. Other types of crises are more commonplace, repeated, and therefore more determinative of the prevailing pattern of expression or repression in a society.

It is, in short, in connection with the threatened riot and the small neighborhood disturbance that civil-liberties policies are tested and proved. It is in conjunction with such immediate events that the "overt act" test and its less stringent form, the "clear and present danger" formula, were primarily relied on. So far as can be seen—certainly if Justice Brennan is a reliable witness—the latter is still used. A speaker who himself incites his followers to riot or pillage can be arrested in his speech when the danger he is igniting seems imminent. Wide discretion remains in the hands of the authorities in interpretation of both the facts in an immediate situation and the rule to be applied to it, yet they are hardly in a position to be arbitrary or even really unpredictable.

But what of speakers or groups whose behavior is lawful, but who provoke violent reaction from bystanders? On the whole, Anglo-American law expects the police to protect the rights of speakers in such situations, as it also their duty to protect the property of newspapers and other media threatened by mobs. Without great explicit concern, however, judges have long acknowledged that a speaker's right to speak at a particular place and time, even if otherwise a proper one, can be abridged in the face of genuine public danger. It would appear that the basic principles are that the authorities have a primary obligation to attempt with all reasonably available resources to protect users of the means of free expression; they may not use the argument of public danger to forbid such expression, but merely to minimize dangers by altering the circumstances of discussion. Thus, in numerous southern civil-rights demonstrations, particular streets and times could be forbidden but not the demonstrations themselves. Similarly—but at lower-court levels—in Chicago demonstrations, followers of Martin Luther King were enjoined to hold only one demonstration a day and to provide twenty-four-hour notice on the grounds that a greater number of demonstrations and those called without advance warning constituted an impossible drain on the police force. When, at about the same time, George Lincoln Rockwell and his neo-Nazi followers announced plans to march through those neighborhoods in Chicago that were predominantly Jewish, they were forbidden to do so during the Jewish High Holy Day period and were enjoined to stay off streets with synagogues, apparently on the theory that such efforts were particularly provocative and therefore potentially dangerous.

Whether such anticipation of merely possible dangers can be the basis for regulation is doubtful; certainly, it would hardly be sufficient grounds to forbid the marches outright. Indeed, even the order limiting the Chicago demonstrations—after a period of time in which they were regularly held so that data purporting to show a crime increase had been assembled—presents novel notions not yet ruled on by the courts.

It is true that, in labor cases, the Justices have sustained regulation of picketing, both as to prohibiting such actions with respect to certain forms of economic relationships—

secondary boycotts and the like—and as to numbers and manner of picketing in lawful demonstrations. But they have done so on the premise that picketing is more than speech, more than an exhortation. Mass picketing, particularly, includes an element of coercion, and a not always disguised hint of violence is implicit in its mere occurrence.

It is by no means unreasonable to argue that even peaceful political marches also contain the identical nonspeech elements. This, however, has not been legally asserted, and there may well be some difference in the proclivity of demonstrators and picketeers to violence, at least in the American experience. Then, too, the Court in the past, has been willing to permit restrictions on union activities that partake of free speech, although preventing similar restrictions on aspects of expression not tainted with a pecuniary touch. In short, peaceable political demonstrations are, on two major counts at least, distinguishable from similar weapons used in an economic struggle.

In Cox, however, Justice Black, speaking for himself and Justice Clark, indicated his belief that all picketing—including political—could be prohibited by a state in a nondiscriminatory statute. Similarly, he suggested that public assemblage was prohibitable subject only to nondiscrimination and absence of censorship. The majority found this at least in part contrary to previous holdings that seemed to preclude total exclusion.[17]

THE COMPETING VALUE OF PRIVACY:
THE RIGHT TO BE FREE FROM OTHERS

Affronts to individual conscience not only take the form of denial of free expression, but also of coercive requirements of enforced declarations. History shows that men have been equally ingenious in this realm, requiring oaths and other affirmations of orthodoxy from reluctant citizenry. In many

---

17.   *Cox v. Louisiana,* 379 U.S. 557 (1965), 579 and 555, n. 13.

ways, being forced to mouth words contrary to one's true beliefs (or in the face of one's doubts or even merely in violation of one's sense of reticence) can be more humiliating, more a violation of the sense of self than merely being forced to remain silent. Even to be coerced into hearing repugnant views can be a trying experience.

Implicit concern with protection from such impositions is found in the constitutional prohibition against religious tests for federal office and the ban on establishment of religion; the prohibition against attainders was held in the post-Civil War period to apply to a loyalty oath intended to proscribe Confederate sympathizers from the legal profession. But the insistence on the right to private nonconformity, "the right to be silent," is on the whole as recent as the right to fulfill the desire to be alone, the right to turn a deaf ear.

The coining of the expression "the right to privacy" and its legal foundations are generally traced to a celebrated law-review article of the same name by Louis Brandeis and Samuel Warren.[18] The quest for such defense of the individual dates back to at least a century previous to the Brandeis–Warren article—to John Stuart Mill and, beyond him, to de Tocqueville, who pointed to the democratic and industrial threat to self-determination, the series of problems now discussed under the rubric "mass society." Formerly, eccentricity in both its positive and negative aspects was buttressed by inherited wealth and position. In a thoroughgoing democratic, capitalistic society, both were likely to be tied to continued public esteem; in a mass society, even millionaires and celebrities could be quickly brought to heel by a predominant train of thought. Conformity, formerly difficult to obtain by force, could be secured through voluntary acquiescence for fear of losing credit, position, or occupation in the light of angry publicity. Artificial legal protection was now necessary to protect not only expression, but

18. Louis Brandeis and Samuel Warren, "The Right to Privacy," *Harvard Law Review*, IV (1890), 193.

also the sense of personal differentiation and self-worth that is the indispensable precondition of self-expression.

Although the article by Brandeis and Warren quickly and quite generally became the subject of considerable attention and approval, its chief and virtually only result for decades was to help permit individuals to sue the mass media for unauthorized use of their pictures, particularly in advertisements. Brandeis' careful argument became another legalized windfall for people fortunate enough to spot use of their likeness by careless ad men.

But the past three decades have seen quite a different drift in legal development, one that has indeed seen the "right to privacy" read into the Constitution as implicit in and even basic to other human rights. Considering the almost totally absent constitutional texts that might serve as a base and the meager handful of cases available for the foundation, the emergence of the right to privacy as a full-fledged basis for decision must be reckoned a phenomenon of modern constitutional law, its implementation a tour de force. Some unfriendly—even a few sympathetic—critics suggest that a legal "boot-strap" operation so relentless and rapid-fire and on so flimsy a legal basis invites both the same criticism and, eventually, the same sort of political and popular repudiation as the runaway laissez-faire Court of the 1920s and 1930s.

The precedents are indeed few, scattered and vague. In West Virginia *v.* Barnette, Justice Jackson suggested some of the themes in language sweeping, arresting, absolute, and clearly overgeneralized. (Jackson, in the Beauharnais Case, was later to note that the constitutional law of free speech was "a subject to the confusion of which I regret to say I have contributed."[19]) The Barnette Case reversed the decision in Minersville School District *v.* Gobitis. The latter case had required school children of Jehovah's Witnesses' background to either salute the flag or be excluded from public schools on the theory that school boards had responsi-

---

19.   343 U.S. 250 (1952), 288.

bility and authority for education in the interest of "national unity" that overrode any plea based on religious objection to worship of a "graven image." In recognizing the Witnesses' claims in Barnette, Jackson did not deal with religion however; rather, he denied the right to "prescribe what shall be orthodox . . . or force citizens to confess by word or act their faith therein."[20] Thus, Barnette is a generalized claim for individual rights to opt out of any socially authorized ritual; it is also a bulwark for claims against the bullying of individuals into conformity. In the light of the overbold assertions of the Barnette case and the resultant confusion, it is perhaps amusing to note that Stone actually had to tone down Jackson's circulating draft!

Much of the same logic applies to the McCollum decision on religious education in the school. Although seriously diluted by the Zorach decision permitting such programs during school hours but off school premises, McCollum showed concern for the sensitivity of the child exposed to the ridicule of fellow students in the type of minority situation—given our pattern of ethnic and religious neighborhoods—that inevitably would be repeated throughout the country and would affect stray adherents to every religious—or irreligious—belief. The same concern is reflected in the New York Regents Case—forbidding secular authorities to compose and then impose prayers—and the Murray and Schempp Cases forbidding Bible reading as a religious exercise in the public schools.

All of this, however, becomes largely a matter of construing dicta, for the fact remains that these are causes involving religious freedom. With the exception of the Barnette Case, they rest on the establishment clause and, although Jackson chose not to base Barnette on the free exercise clause, religious conviction remains an element in the case.

Indeed, in the clearest confrontation on the issue of

---

20.   319 U.S. 624 (1943), 642.

privacy, the Capital-Transit Case, a majority found it permissible for the Washington bus lines to pipe music and commercials to a semicaptive audience. The question of whether it would be permissible to subject the traveler to political opinion, it was intimated, would be answered differently. (There are alternatives to public transportation, as transit companies have found to their dismay.) Public pressure forced discontinuance of the practice, but the significant fact is that the Justices felt, in these circumstances at least, that it was not their function to interfere, even in the name of privacy.

Even more strikingly, the same Court—with only one change in personnel—that proclaimed the constitutional right of privacy sharply delimited the use of suits for damages for invasion of privacy as developed in response to the Brandeis appeal. The case involved a family held at gunpoint by a group of criminals. Sometime later, a fictionalized movie appeared; *Life* magazine chose to cover this in detail, with a story identifying the family and drawing explicit parallels. Pointing to the family's efforts to avoid publicity, the lapse of time, and the possibility of confusion of movie details with the actual experiences, the Hills sued under a New York statute. The Supreme Court applied its *New York Times* reasoning, holding that comment on newsworthy individuals is not restricted in time, and no monetary penalties could be assessed in the absence of a reckless disregard for truth.

In a collision between media comment and the claim for a private right to avoid public attention, the Court chose to expand still more its recent emphasis on liberation of comment. This partly reflects the basic contradiction in the notion of a suit for damages to vindicate a desire for publicity, so that those really seeking privacy are the least likely to use the remedy. More than that, it illustrates the vagueness of the concept of privacy and the fact that this new, strange, and mysterious constitutional doctrine has yet to become rooted in social reality and concrete decision. What is meant by it is not clear, but it isn't what it used to be.

FEDERAL STANDARDS AND STATE ACTION

We have already summarized the development of political liberty as a process of nationalizing standards of freedom enforcible in federal courts. But, within this development, there is yet another—the direct intrusion of federal standards on state officials exercising discretion. To some extent, certainly, state officials benefit from the Court's ruling on exemption from libel; however, it is clear that the recent rulings do not provide appreciably greater exemption for state officials, who have always been accorded wide discretion under the defense of privileged comment in libel. At the same time, the Bond decision and such legislative committee cases as the Gibson Case allow federal control over state legislatures in an operative rather than merely legislative capacity, whereas a decade or so ago, no control would have been allowed under the doctrine of "political question." Nonetheless, the state official remains remarkably free to use his power in a manner independent of any court control— as prosecutor Garrison has been demonstrating in his "investigation" of the Kennedy assassination; this, after all, is the price of federalism.

What, however, most clearly strains and tests the bounds of our dual government is when local officials not only use their powers to deliberately thwart federal law, but also to perpetrate illegal acts. We have already referred to this problem in Chapter 3. Here, we may note that this issue of "the pirate state" sometimes is resolved by waiting until the federal right becomes manifest or by removing the case to a federal court, invoking such principles as the "void on its face" doctrine to protect the citizenry of the state—or its visitors—from maltreatment by a government.

But the machinery of the state may be used to create a wrong by merely threatening. A civil rights worker can be harassed by requiring him to defend himself against ridiculous charges that are dropped at the end of the summer. In Dombrowski *v.* Pfister, the Supreme Court decided that federal courts could issue injunctions to stay state action where the result of the state proceedings was to thwart free expression protected by the federal constitution and the purpose of the proceedings was deliberately to extinguish or diminish the federal right. Such action had been established in commercial cases in Ex Parte Young, but Dombrowski extended the practice to the domain of personal liberty.[21]

Thus, procedurally and substantially, the nationwide scope of First Amendment rights has been expanded.

ONE ISSUE OR MANY: A METHODOLOGICAL PROBLEM

In recent years, students of the judicial process have found that the Justices divide pretty much the same no matter what the civil-liberties question. This does not mean that the vote is always identical; far from it. This depends on the dimensions of the case; even some civil-liberties situations produce unanimous Courts. What it does seem to mean is that, if cases show Justice Douglas more friendly to civil liberties than Justice Harlan, and we know Harlan voted for a claimed right, we can deduce that Douglas did too—or conversely, assuming Douglas voted negatively.

All of this can be deduced verbally or qualitatively of course, but current efforts attempt to do so precisely and

---

21. Dombrowski, in a related action, claimed that not only did state officials conspire to harass him, but also that Senator Eastland and the staff of a Senate committee responsible to him issued deliberately damaging and false statements. The Supreme Court found that, since the statements were made in an official capacity, the Senator did not need to defend the charge at all and that the staff could be brought to suit, but under the strong doctrine of privilege of *Barr v. Matteo*.

mathematically so as to reduce the subjective factor involved in picking the issues and cases. One such method is Guttman Scalogram analysis, where an attempt is made to array both the cases and the Justices in order of intensity, moving from case to case in a serial order as they present more severe or less severe problems of liberty, with the Justices arrayed in their inclination to support claims of expression.[22]

By and large, this method—as well as more complex efforts, usually employing factor analysis or some variant— has tended to suggest that the Justices can be so ranked. Since there are, in fact, subjective elements and rival approaches on small matters of technique, some deviations appear, but by and large the findings of this more technical literature comport well but are not identical with the general repute of the Justices. The findings also comply with the standards conventionally regarded as indicating unidimensionality, that is, suggesting that the Justices regard the problem the same way, agreeing on which cases are more severe than others but disagreeing as to where the line between permissible and impermissible action is to be drawn.

There are at least four general possible explanations of the findings over and above the possibility of unique positions held by the Justices. One is that the issues are by nature unidimensional—that is, a person who is permissive in obscenity cases must logically be a "liberal" on internal security cases. The issues may also be sociologically or culturally related. That is to say, certain groups may hold these values, which are not logically interrelated. Because Justices are drawn from a narrow range of groups, they may consequently reflect the peculiar social values of these social or cultural ambiences with their minor variations. It is also possible to argue that the Justices are in fact selected precisely to repre-

22. See Glendon Schubert, *The Judicial Mind* (Evanston, Ill.: Northwestern University Press, 1965); Schubert, *Judicial Behavior* (Chicago: Rand-McNally, 1964), pp. 306–52; and Joseph Tannenhaus, "Cumulative Scaling of Judicial Decisions," *Harvard Review*, LXXIX (1966), 1551.

sent their type of point of view. Presidents and other poli-
ticians scrutinize the situation and find some who represent
some gap in representation generally along a continuum.
Finally, it must be realized that the processes of Court action
encourage undimensionality. The vote on a case is not just a
casual response on a stray poll. There has been considerable
literature on how often discussion in conference changes
votes. There is one thing that discussion almost certainly
must do and that is to sensitize the Justices to a common
appreciation of what are the tough and the easy cases.

I would argue that, in fact, none of these explanations is
a total explanation and that really all play a role. (However,
I doubt if the explanation of selectivity is an important one
since I doubt that prior scrutiny is or can be that exacting.)
It seems to me that there are series of probabilities operative
here. There is a logic to civil-liberties positions that leads to
but does not compel congruent positions on each scale. This
is true for individuals and for the groups from which they
derive. Assuming average deviation from these interrelated
positions—and true deviants are not likely to have a reputation for "judicial temperament" or the minimum political
backing for selection—we would not get extensive crossovers
of position in a nine-man body. Discussion and emphasis on
rationalization would bring out the need for congruent approaches and tend to unite the Justices on perspective or
orientation. The legal process emphasizes and rewards the
type of men who exemplify logical interrelatedness.

Some have contended that the use of broad, semilegal
classifications (semilegal in this instance, nonlegal in others)
to successfully classify judges' differences either debunks law
or replaces it or both. We need not worry about the niceties
of judicial rationalization if we know whether the judges are
"prodefendant" in different degree rather than most sensitive to the facts of guilt or innocence. It is, perhaps, not accidental that such interpretations come more often from critics
of current efforts than from defenders, for they misconceive

both the current situation and the ultimate potentialities of the techniques in question.

Let us assume the methods involved were more firmly established than they are. (Not only are there—as usual in scientific inquiry disagreements about specific procedures, but also the subjectively controllable elements are acknowledged to be considerable to the point of quite possibly vitiating conclusions.) Let us assume the results were less unequivocal than they are. (A number of individual votes have not, in fact, fitted the schematic arrangement, but the deviations have been within the conventionally established criteria for error—criteria that were chosen arbitrarily and may have no particular empirical meaning. Justice Black's recent vagaries will surely disorder many an ordered arrangement.) This would still not establish the explanation involved as the correct one; indeed, it is a peculiarity of current arraying techniques that they give us no notion—however artificial— of probability of correctness.

More to the point is the fact that relational findings— how each Justice comports with others—is not a determinative finding at all. There are many ways of being "liberal" on obscenity; the Supreme Court has proven this in a very short number of years. The translation of general attitude to specific vote seems to involve an intermediate process involving more general decision rules that vary from domain to domain. It would appear—at least from present potentialities—that Justices will still profit from legal training and need not throw away their books. At the present time, the study of judicial behavior offers classification of voting, not behavioral explanation. Even if a major breakthrough occurs, it will be explanation of a particular type that will ensue, leaving virtually untouched the need for legal and social justification of decisions.

5

The Power of the Court

PRELIMINARY REMARKS

Perhaps a decade ago, this discussion might have properly stopped here. But, in recent years, a growing call has been heard for emphasis on the empirical consequences of legal decisions—not merely on the theoretical and logical aspects of a self-contained legal system, but also on the impact of the system on a broader society. Such an approach is not totally unknown to older writers; it can, for instance, be found in such observations as Holmes' famous predictive theory of law: "The prophecies of what the courts will do in fact and nothing more pretentious are what I mean by law."[1] Others, such as Henry Edgerton and Underhill Moore made more direct pleas for such an approach and conspicuously inaugurated research of their own to deal with

---

1. Oliver Wendell Holmes, "The Path of the Law," *Collected Legal Papers* (Boston: Harcourt, Brace & Howe, 1920), p. 173.

the impact of "law in action." These were generally isolated efforts, however, whereas more recently, among both legal scholars and social scientists interested in law, there has been a growing chorus of emphasis on the desirability of such research. But that chorus, like Mark Twain's commentators on the weather, has generally emphasized more the need for action than actually contributed to a remedy.

Nor is that surprising—and hardly a reflection on current efforts—for impact studies present grave problems in research and require vast resources seldom available. Even conceptually, the problem of impact measurement presents grave difficulties hardly resolved by the usual efforts at studying the immediate aftermath of some dramatic event or decision. (Even the most careful study cannot establish whether alleged changes were not merely coincidentally but actually consequentially related.) Even such relatively modest slice-of-life studies as public-opinion surveys normally require support from a foundation or governmental agency; yet, in truth, they are only indices of possible impact rather than an evaluation of effectiveness itself. In short, these normal approaches, though excellent research strategies, not only provide limited information, but also require extensive and expensive efforts from researchers.

This chapter will attempt a summary of available or readily obtainable information on the effectiveness of the Supreme Court on political freedom. It is almost redundant to add that this constitutes an exploratory statement, in many ways as much an inquiry into methods of answering such a question as it is an answer itself.

THE INCIDENCE OF JUDICIAL REVIEW

The first approach to the problem will be one essayed by Judge Edgerton in his celebrated essay, "The Incidence of Judicial Control Over Congress." He noted that a true debit-and-credit analysis of Court action would involve such matters as the effect of review on congressional legislation, including "the number and character of the acts which Congress has been deterred from enacting or encouraged to enact,"[2] political initiative of masses and leaders, and judicial action in other courts as a consequence of Supreme Court action or its refusal to review. But Judge Edgerton did not undertake this extensive task, confining himself to the nonetheless broad one of meticulously evaluating in social terms the consequences of each instance of judicial invalidation of congressional actions to 1933. (To avoid accusations of political motivation, the judge did not comment on cases decided in the four years of the New Deal that had already become a matter of record prior to the original publication of the essay.) "I am concerned only with the practical effects of the nullifying decisions. Whose interests, individual or social do they protect; and conversely whose ox is gored?"[3] Even this more limited task involved the then law professor from 1922 through 1936.

We need not occupy ourselves exhaustively with his conclusions: that the primary effect of Court action was to protect business at the expense of majority interests; that Negroes and Chinese were protected from some specific discriminatory statutes but that these were limited in scope and application, whereas protection of Negroes' voting rights and broad vindication of their liberties had actually been hampered by the Court; and that laboring interests had been ignored or thwarted through the years. These generalizations

---

2. Henry Edgerton, *Selected Essays in Constitutional Law* (Brooklyn: Foundation Press, 1938), pp. 793–4. There is some evidence that writers —not excluding myself—have exaggerated the effect on Congress of previous judicial decisions. See Harry Stumpf, "Congressional Response to Supreme Court Rulings," *Journal of Public Law*, XIV (1966), 377. A more complex but quite compatible conclusion emerges from Donald Morgan, *Congress and the Constitution* (Cambridge, Mass.: Harvard University Press, 1966).

3. Edgerton, p. 795.

obviously have little application to the last three decades, which can in many respects be regarded as almost compensatory to what had previously occurred.

More to the point are his findings with respect to political freedom. He found that no case involving speech, press, and assembly resulted in its protection. Indeed, only a handful of cases (seven) really involved the Bill of Rights and in highly limited ways, most relating to criminal-trial procedures. The one case contributing to political liberty in that whole period was Ex Parte Garland, which held invalid a congressional requirement that attorneys practicing in federal courts take an oath of nonparticipation in a rebellion against the United States. Edgerton concludes that, in any event, this would have been quickly repealed as Civil War tensions declined. He, therefore, found no substantive contribution to freedom of expression on the part of the Court in its first 148 years.[4]

A decade and a half later, Richard Sklar consciously followed Judge Edgerton's approach, and, although his conclusions are somewhat different, as required in part by the passage of time, they sound equally odd to the present-day ear: "The Court has shown less concern for values of free speech than for those of order. . . . As between dissidents of the right and those of the left, the statistics show a marked advantage for the right."[5] These differences are, in fact, a consequence of a different attitude on freedom of speech dur-

----

4. In a seminar paper at the University of Minnesota, Winter, 1966, Mr. Theodore Pedeliski maintained that Edgerton's method of dealing with the precise case necessarily minimizes the effect of a judicial decision. My own inspection of Edgerton's case evaluations suggests, at a minimum, that the judge was not generous in his ascription of contributions by the judiciary. Thus Boyd *v.* United States, the bedrock of developments in search and seizure, confessions, and similar issues that are at this writing so controversial, is described as protecting "practically nothing except the interests of smugglers." (Edgerton, p. 797).

5. Richard Sklar, "The Fiction of the First Freedom," *Western Political Quarterly,* VI (June, 1953), 318.

ing World War I and in subsequent years, for different types of defendants were involved in the different periods.

Thus, both Edgerton and Sklar suggest that some important differences have taken place in Court action, for today it is common to hear the complaint of Judge Edward Dumbauld, who, as early as 1950, suggested that only "picketers, prisoners, proselyters, publicans . . . and pigmented portions of the population" could gain Court attention.[6]

If one applied the same test as Edgerton, there would be little enough indication of any change. It appears that judicial invalidation of congressional action remains relatively infrequent (see Table 5–1). Apparently, the Court prefers to achieve its results in political matters through either such methods of statutory interpretation—as urged by Hand and Frankfurter—or individualistic or due process grounds. (Thus, in the Aptheker Case, the Court pro-offered a complete rationale on abridgement of freedom of association only to decide in the end that the action violated the Fifth Amendment. Only in the Lamont Case in 1965 was a judgment of violation of the First Amendment by Congress made, albeit unanimously.)

Table 5–1—The Incidence of Judicial Invalidation of Congressional Action Relating to Political Freedom

	1789–1867	1868–1899	1900–1949	1950–1964	1964–1966
First Amendment	0	0	0	0	1
Other Political Rights	(1)	1	1	1	1

Derived from Legislative Reference Service, *The Constitution of the United States* (Washington: Government Printing Office, 1964), pp. 1387 ff.

Certainly the slight increase in frequency represented in Table 5–1 (note differing time lapses) would not justify discussion of a radical shift in the Court role. The most conspicuous shift, in fact, has occurred in other areas—invalidation of state and local legislation. (See Table 5–2.)

---

6. Edward Dumbauld, "Judicial Review and Popular Sovereignty," *University of Pennsylvania Law Review*, XCIX (1950), 201.

Table 5–2—Cases in which State Legislation Was Invalidated, 1789–1963

	1789–1867	1868–1899	1900–1923	1924–1949	1950–1963
Total Cases	25	112	180	209	102
First Amendment Political Cases	0	0	0	15	8
Other Political Cases	1	1	3	3	8
Communications Cases (Other than Political)	0	6	6	2	0

Derived from *The Constitution of the United States* (1964), pp. 1405 ff.

As can be seen both absolutely and relatively, the Court has recently tended to give more consideration to political freedoms. And this tendency has been consistently increasing. Thus, in the 1963–1964 term, fifteen invalidations took place with twelve political decisions in broad terms, and fully five of them involved First Amendment freedoms.

The same trend is evident in the data on invalidation of municipal ordinances. (See Table 5–3.)

Table 5–3—Cases in which Municipal Ordinances Were Invalidated Respecting Political Freedom, 1789–1963

	1789–1828	1829–1899	1900–1923	1924–1949	1950–1963
Total	0	12	34	24	13
First Amendment Cases	0	0	0	12	6
Other Political Cases	0	0	0	0	1
Communications Cases	0	1	3	0	0

Derived from *The Constitution of the United States,* pp. 1522 ff.

THE BENEFICIARIES OF INVALIDATION

The range of groups so benefited does, in fact, indicate a definite shift to the defense of leftists, although rightists also were recently benefited. The range of groups is in fact pronounced, encompassing left to right as well as weak to the strong. A major beneficiary, for example, has been the mass media, particularly the affluent newspapers and magazines who have been insulated from repressive state measures, libel suits by individuals, and, most recently, many suits based on

claims of privacy through partial or complete invalidation
of state and municipal regulations. (See Table 5–4).

**Table 5–4—Groups Benefited By Invalidations of Legislation
Affecting Political Rights, 1789–1963**

Civil War Confederates	2	Religious Dissenters	12
Teachers	3	*Negroes	4
Left-Wing Advocates	8	General Organizations and	
Right-Wing Racists	3	Rights to Membership	7
Mass-Circulation Press	3	Alleged Pornographic	
Pamphleteers and Circulators		Literature and Movies	6
of Leaflets	11	Atheists	1
Labor	4	Aliens	2

* Does not include right-to-vote or equal-facilities cases.
Derived from *The Constitution of the United States*, pp. 1387ff, 1405ff, and 1522ff.

Yet, the consequences of the exertion of judicial review
of legislation cannot be deemed very impressive. The average
number of invalidations of all types of legislation since 1924
has been a little more than one a year. Since 1950, this has
radically increased in a relative sense, but two invalidations
a year (the approximate average in that period) cannot be
deemed an awesome figure. Even the totals of the past three
or four years—a period regarded as one of the two most
active in history—averaged only three a year. Those three
instances covering the entire gamut of legislation obviously
would be insufficient by themselves to control all levels of
government in relation to political freedom.

OTHER MEANS OF CONTROL

Judicial invalidation of legislation is hardly the only
means by which the judiciary influences political life. It does
not even exhaust the practices known as judicial review,
which are regarded as a uniquely distinguishing feature of
the American legal order. Invalidation of executive actions
on constitutional grounds—whether the action is on the national or state level—or reversal of judicial decisions on that
basis are all means of judicial power that are less ostentatious
in use and more assimilated to the traditional legal role.

Further, statutory interpretation to avoid the issue of constitutionality has long been recognized as a potent weapon, for
severe recasting may be necessary to "save" a constitutionally
doubtful bit of legislation. Even simple statutory interpretation must be given its due; armed only with this weapon, the
British judiciary has managed to play a major role in the
political life of the country. The impact of the United States
Supreme Court on civil liberties cannot therefore be meas-
ured mainly in terms of laws declared unconstitutional.
More properly, it must include an assessment of all its actions
pro and con and the impact of each, no matter what the legal
basis or the technique employed. Edgerton himself has a
long and thoughtful discussion of some of the difficulties so
raise.

A second consideration also intrudes itself. Legal decisions are never single acts, political events, or assertions. In
form and intent, they are presumed to be generalized assertions of principle intended to have radiating consequences.
Judiciary policy is claimed to be a cumulative process—the
accretion of precedent upon precedent. Thus, the radiating
effects of a decision must also be considered, as "multiplier
effects" may be felt throughout a broadly dispersed legal
order.

Both of these aspects will concern us. How many decisions of various kinds do indeed influence the course of
political freedom? How much do decisions so rendered re-
verberate through our constitutional order? It is to these two
questions that we now turn.

In attempting to assess the effort exerted by the Court—
the impact or compliance potential as it were—preoccupation with well-known cases in which the overt legal issue is
expression seems inadequate; at the very least, one can say
that it is an approach that has been overused.

Accordingly, the effort here will be to deal in less usual
ways with two years of Court action. The 1963 and 1964
terms will be analyzed and cases will be classified not in

terms of constitutional or legal categories, but in terms of impact. A decision inhibiting or punishing expression will be included no matter how it arises; thus, labor picketing and sit-in cases are included as well as a case involving a suit to disbar an attorney for advising his client 'to leave her husband and others withdrawing telephone service from gamblers. All such cases docketed (and those on the miscellaneous docket in which full opinions were filed) will then be classified in terms of whether the indicated result favored an increase in expression or not—a question answered as narrowly as possible. A decision called "unfavorable to expression" is not conceived of as necessarily undesirable. Indeed, the attempt here is to avoid deciding on desirability or what is good doctrine. Thus the Court upheld the right of a school board to require certification that school premises rented out for meetings would not knowingly be used for illegal purposes; this would be classified as a restrictive or unfavorable case, although I personally have no doubt that this was the proper decision. Similarly, a state prohibition on billboards upheld by the Court will appear as a restrictive decision, although other—and, to me, as to the judges, overwhelmingly more significant—nonexpression values are present.

In treating these two terms of the Court in such stark behavioristic terms—to supplement our more extensive qualitative discussion—some modification proves necessary. In the first place, the Court, in the course of a single term, may decide only to decide a case without reaching a final disposition. In such a case, it would appear improper to treat this as a neutral action, since immediate dismissal or refusal to hear the case was the alternative. Accordingly, we will treat a decision to review a restrictive decision as favorable in a preliminary way, whereas the decision to review a favorable lower-court decision will be listed as partially or provisionally unfavorable.

Further, real-life cases often present not so much a

question of whether expression shall be upheld, but what kind of expression shall be upheld where there is a collision. Thus, the Court has been called to decide on the propriety of sit-ins at a church and at public meetings, where the demonstrators deliberately created a disturbance effectively thwarting the expression of the original assemblage. Such cases are treated separately here. (See Table 5–5.)

Table 5–5—Supreme Court Resolution of Cases Involving Freedom of Expression (By Source of Appeal and Year)

	1963			1964		
	Federal Case	State Case	All	Federal Case	State Case	All
Favorable	10	24	34	13	29	42
Favorable (procedural)	3	5	8	3	6	9
Unfavorable	13	11	24	14	19	33
Unfavorable (procedural)	2	0	2	0	0	0
Collision of rights	2	1	3	0	4	4
No action	5	4	9	3	10	13
Total	35	45	80	33	68	107

What emerges from this compilation? In the first place, the number of cases involved is not great, considering that our definition of type of case treated is very broad and our analyzed sample includes many cases disposed of by dismissal of appeal or denial of *certiorari* with only cursory treatment and no or little explanation. If these two sessions are deemed typical, the Court acts on less than one hundred cases (exclusive of those in the miscellaneous docket, which is largely composed of criminal cases in any event). Further, although the Warren Court is comfortably more prone to find in favor of than against a claimed liberty, the net difference is not pronouncedly large, the deviation from 50 percent to 50 percent disposition being relatively small.

On the other hand, the Court not only reviews more cases originating from the state and local level than it does federal cases affecting expression, but also it more often reverses state than federal decisions. This finding is perhaps, legally speaking, surprising, in view of the principles of state autonomy and standards of federalism and the supposedly greater supervisory power of the Supreme Court over federal courts. But it will hardly surprise those conversant with the realities of civil liberties. The tough cases raising issues of fluctuating legal standards or highly subjective judgments generally originate in local transactions; and, in any event, state courts are less sensitive to federal standards. This latter factor has been even more prominent in recent years when some southern courts have seemingly been willing to act in a manner that they must have assumed would lead to reversal. Nonetheless, the numbers, even though swelled by the sit-in-cases, that were at their peak in these two terms, hardly are overwhelming.

THE NATURAL INCREASE OF PRECEDENTS

The significance of Court decisions are, however, not just unique events, but also precedents. How much must we inflate each decision? What "multiplier effect" may each decision have? To determine this on the basis of a recent decision is inadequate, for diffusion of opinion is a slow process. Accordingly, the groups of cases used to evaluate the cumulative effects of a decision is the body of invalidating decisions made by the Court during the period.

Shephard's Citations (which comprehensively lists later citations of cases) has been consulted in each instance, with citations from federal courts cumulated by type of citation listed—followed, distinguished, and so forth. Since the listing of citations made by federal courts includes the specific points for which the case is cited, I have omitted those where the listing clearly involves a legal point not involving expression, for example, a matter of legal procedure. All general citations or ambiguous headings are included. Since state-court citations of Supreme Court cases are classified neither by legal point involved nor by what type of precedent value is attached to the case, a simple total of all citations is the sole possibility short of the exhausting business of tracking down diverse state cases. (See Tables 5–6 and 5–7.)

Table 5–6—Frequency of Citations By Various Courts of Forty Supreme Court Decisions (1867–1958) Invalidating Laws on a Free-Expression Basis

	Supreme Court	Other Federal Courts	Total of All State Courts	All
Range of number of citations	2–144	2–190	6–370	19–565
Mean number of citations	41	37	74	152

Derived from *Shephard's Citations* through 1966. List of cases derived from *United States Constitution Annotated.*

Table 5–7—Distribution of Citations in Forty Free-Expression Cases By Type of Use Given in the Supreme Court and Other Federal Courts

	SUPREME COURT		OTHER FEDERAL COURTS	
	Number of Cities	Percent	Cities Number of	Percent
Controlling or Followed	48	2.9	44	3.0
Distinguished, Overruled, or Questioned	54	3.3	108	7.3
Sample Cite or Explained	1040	62.7	1136	77.6
Justified	517	31.2	176	12.0
Total	1659		1465	

Derived from *Shephard's Citations* through 1966. List of cases derived from *United States Constitution Annotated.*

In both instances, federal and state, it appears there has been a tendency to overemphasize the precedent value of cases. This is at least true in the sense of attributing significant specific, causal effects to previous cases, of describing previous decisions as "controlling" later ones. Especially if we turn from the figures on mere citation to the "followed" data with regard to federal courts, it becomes obvious that such compellingness is not standard. Even if one were to assume that, in all instances in which a federal court noted it was following a precedent, it did so with a consciousness of no option, the presence of such a consciousness occurs only in a small fraction of the total number of cases. The impression that only a few cases is precedent controlling might possibly be altered if *Shephard's* provided a breakdown for state citations similar to the federal breakdown. Perhaps the bulk of state court citations are preemptory dispositions on the basis of Supreme Court reasoning. This is within the realm of possibility, although the logic of court relationships and the opinions of writers on the judicial process suggest the opposite. An informal follow-up on some of the cases in the sample here also does not suggest such a pattern; state citations are seemingly as randomly employed as federal. It is also possible to speculate that the effects of a decision are extrajudicial, that lawyers and administrators pay more attention to precedent value than judges, but this is at best problematic and unconvincing.

Does this then suggest that legalities play little role in disposing of questions of right of expression, that the Supreme Court is deluding us in carrying out this function? It would appear that Court influence is something a bit more diffuse, less tight, more subtle, and yet real. By and large, lower-court judges could not remain thoroughly informed on all the day-to-day bread-and-butter matters that come before them. For all the interest in such matters in the legal profession, the number of attorneys who specialize in the area of expression is small. Outside the ACLU staff and that of similar organizations, such attorneys would tend to be narrower specialists—copyright experts, for example, or specialists in libel law. In short, neither professional legal career patterns nor day-to-day judicial experience are likely to contribute to the development of judges as minutely concerned with freedom of expression as Supreme Court Justices must be. (The exceptions in the lower courts have almost always been drawn from academia rather than the ranks of the practitioner.) The briefs before even relatively high-level

courts are not always of high quality nor necessarily of pin-
point accuracy in their legal acumen.[7] Chance all too often
dictates who the lawyer pleading the case is and what his
interests and skills are.

But, in a general way, the major lines of Supreme Court
reasoning are likely to filter through. Newspaper coverage;
journal articles; the cumulative effect of the briefs, which
may be quite good as well as quite bad; the reading of those
cases or extracts from such cases as emerge as crucial from
the legal argument; the research of the judge who is responsible for the major drafting of the opinion—all have conscious
or subliminal effect on the end product. Legal citation is not
the only form of imitation nor the only index of influence,
nor does a single case usually tell as much about the direction
of the law as the cumulative effect of a line of decisions,
especially with a dispersion of extreme cases that help de-
limit the minimum and maximum lines of decisions. The
very climate and disposition of Supreme Court opinion, its
fundamental attitude toward a process or series of events,
may also be a better prognosticator of future decision than
narrow reading of particular cases. The mood of the law may
be its life force rather than its letter, although the latter
provides the perimeters of the former.

Such notions have been embraced by such divergent
authorities as Learned Hand and Hugo Black and developed
in more systematic form—based on organizational theory—
by Martin Shapiro.[8]

It is, for example, highly suggestive to look at the two
terms of the Supreme Court we have previously analyzed in
precisely such broader terms. When we treated the net ad-

---

7. Karl Llewellyn reported that his investigation of appellate briefs indi-
    cated only semi-competence. See *The Common Law Tradition: Decid-
    ing Appeals* (Boston: Little, Brown & Co., 1960), p. 30.
8. Hand, *The Bill of Rights*, pp. 18–27; Hugo Black in *Cox* v. *Louisiana;*
    Martin Shapiro, "Stability and Change in Judicial Decision-making:
    Incrementalism or Stare Decisis," *Law in Transition Quarterly*, II
    (1965), 134.

vantage for expression as emerging from some sort of ratio or difference between favorable and unfavorable decisions, a respectable but thin margin emerged. A more emphatic result emerges if we compare the decisions reached at lower courts with Supreme Court actions.

During the two year period covered, the Supreme Court chose to review only two cases where the lower courts' decisions had *favored* the right of expression. In one instance, United States *v.* Johnson, the facts, the novelty, and the sensitivity of the issue required review. (A Congressman was convicted of taking a bribe to make a speech in Congress; it had been held that the evidence as to the context and motive of speeches in Congress was in violation of constitutional protection of legislative freedom of speech. Ultimately, the Court upheld congressional immunity.) In Linn *v.* United Plant Guard Workers, however, the Court construed the rights of a speaker more narrowly than the lower court had— but this by only a 5–4 margin. In all other instances (indeed, since the decision in Linn was finally reached in 1966, we may even say with greater exactitude, in all instances) during two full terms, the Supreme Court decided every case involving expression as favorably as or more favorably than the unit from which the decision was appealed.

Such cues, the broad drift of opinion, joined with crucial and dramatic decisions, highlight the tendency of doctrine. Where the law is heading is, we may speculate, as good or better a focus for decision for lower judges than black-letter parsing. When the tendency was as clear and marked in the direction of liberalization as during this two-year term, individual precedents might well take a back seat. Distinctive areas of progress and some clues as to just how far liberalization would proceed would then be gleaned from the tenor of decisions rather than the principles or rules. Individual precedents, then, would serve as boundaries more than as routes.

THE VIEW FROM THE SOCIETAL LEVEL

There is, of course, another way of viewing impact—not so much of cumulative actions and imposed restraints but of direct curtailment or control of others. It is to this dimension that we now turn.

The most direct influence of legal decisions is on the mass printed media. Libel laws and decisions, efforts at censorship, and the style and tone of governmental activity are of great concern to newspapers and magazines of comment. Like the rest of the communications industry, they also exhibit a narcissistic self-concern that makes them especially vulnerable to pressure and sensitive to nuances of approval and disapproval.

THE PRINTED MEDIA AND THE IMPRINT OF THE COURT

The printed word remains the great conduit of interpretative comment and opinion formation. The aural media —especially television—are relied upon for immediate information; but the limits of coverage potential and the excessive timidity of an industry anxious to avoid all controversy for both political and pecuniary motives has left the newspaper the elite mode of news interpretation.

At the same time, the printed media uniquely retain a preoccupation with political and social concerns; they remain centered on informational functions, whereas the visual-aural media are largely entertainment centered. Although the tradition of centuries and the development of semiprofessional craft standards emphasizing reporter obligations is often cant rather than reality such tradition as carries over elsewhere is completely derivative and palid.

Newspapers, magazines, and books, then, by tradition carry on functions that at least theoretically require them to cover events that make the describer vulnerable to charges of error; that coverage also is expected to be sufficiently searching to require some risk. All too often—probably in the majority of run-of-the-mill libel cases—routine negligence in reporting simple facts causes damage suits. But, at least mythologically and often enough in actuality, the collision of the communications industry with the machinery of law has come as a consequence of criticizing or even exposing the conduct of the rich and powerful. Not only libel suits, but also overt or ingenious censorship, punitive tax laws, and efforts at curtailment of distribution are means by which the media may be threatened or punished.

The focal, salient nature of the printed word makes the industry a prime and visible target. Almost invariably, governmental repressive actions that were based on disagreement in policy or as a consequence of public criticism of an officeholder's conduct have been aimed at newspapers or, much less frequently, other forms of publishing; seldom are other mass media involved. Studies such as the Shulman-Clark investigation of litigation in Connecticut indicate that libel, for example, is a comparatively rare form of legal action and that, when it occurs, it is usually aimed at the press.[9] The verdicts involved are relatively chancey—about as likely to favor the defendant as the plaintiff even in cases finally reaching the jury.[10] The amounts involved in most instances have been potentially serious if repeated in other cases but not generally hampering; there is a quality to the awards that suggests lump-sum thinking analogous to taking out life insurance, modified only by a tendency to arbitrate by dividing disputed sums. The amounts of awards had stayed remarkably stable for a quarter-century or longer—at a maximum of about $100,000[11]—until recent sensational figures in a number of well-publicized cases, which involve initial

---

9. Charles Clark and Harry Shulman, *A Study of Law Administration in Connecticut* (New York: Oxford University Press, 1937), pp. 28, 45.
10. Clark and Shulman, p. 31. Fifty-eight per cent of the verdicts reached were for the plaintiff, 42 per cent for the defendant.
11. See Richard McCormick, "Measure of Damages for Defamation," *North Carolina Law Review*, XII (1934), 148–50. A good deal of this has been rendered obsolete by the development of libel insurance.

awards by juries of sums up to and exceeding $1,000,000. Of course, as the case of Congressman Adam Clayton Powell rather dramatically illustrated, it is one thing to get a jury award and another to collect it. Not only is there a problem of evasion of payment or lack of assets to meet it, but also more realistic and central for awards against newspapers is the power of judges (appellate judges as well as the trial judge) to alter the verdict. Although theoretically awards can also be increased, in practice judges are extremely reluctant to do so, so that the appellate and settlement process is one of scaling down jury verdicts.[12]

Thus, the judiciary retains firm control both of governmental action against the major news and information media and of obvious and direct individual initiative to curtail content. Under the First Amendment, the exercise of any governmental authority relative to the press can be called into account, and the common-law control by judges in libel cases can be decisive.

An apparent loophole in this control became visible in recent years. A plaintiff may take advantage of national circulation, however limited, of publications to file multiple suits for damages in all locales where they are found; additionally, where the basis of alleged damage is in reality disagreement about political evaluations, he may shop for a locality where congenial juries and judges are likely to favor him. The latter possibility has been implicit in our federal order and historically was treated as inevitable; abolitionists got short shrift from southern juries and judges, whereas slave owners found some states totally unsympathetic, with no redress from the judiciary. Until the 1920s, the federal judiciary did not concern itself with such questions, and, until the *New York Times* Case, it had no leverage in such

---

12. Of McCormick's compilation of published verdicts in the period 1928–1932, eleven of forty-three resulted in change at the appellate level; in all instances but one, the result was a reduction in the amount awarded; of twenty-six identifiable defendants, twelve were newspapers.

tort proceedings unless highly unusual circumstances were present. That momentous decision also provided a more effective answer to the dangers of multiple suits as well.

Examples of both potentials are available. During the post-World War II period, ex-Congressman Martin Sweeney filed somewhere between seventy-five to four hundred suits against columnist Drew Pearson for alleging that Sweeney was anti-Semitic. Sweeney abandoned the field after a few adverse verdicts, based on quite divergent and even contradictory grounds, in various courts.[13] But it seems likely, given the somewhat inferential nature of the charge, that he should have prevailed in some jurisdiction had he persisted. In any event, the trials had a necessarily punitive nature in costs to the defense. Of course, plaintiff costs and the plain implications of such a series of suits—with probably negative reaction by those permitted to learn of the tactic—constituted strong deterrents.

But instances of the problem of regional bias or super-convenient forums were more clearcut and potentially more repressive; the *Times* Case itself was only the most dramatic example. In the Walker Case, the Associated Press was found to have acted with malice (legal equivalent of "with reckless disregard for the truth") in its coverage of the activities of General Walker during the integration of the University of Mississippi. Associated Press dispatches suggested that the former Army Commander had "harangued the crowd," urged violence, and had sought to lead the student resisters, whereas Walker apparently established that his speeches were vaguely exhortatory and patriotic. The jury had its normally difficult and subjective balancing act to perform here, as in many defamation cases, so that it is bootless and unfair to criticize it for finding for the General. In view of the facts that Walker had traveled many miles and states to thrust himself into the situation and chose to address the crowd,

13. See David Riesman, "Democracy and Defamation," *Columbia Law Review*, XLII (1942), 1291 *ff.*

as well as the difficulties of press coverage of mob situations, it is difficult to see justification for the malice finding except in terms of Confederate revenge on irritating, snooping Yankee reporters. (The Louisiana courts, however, indicated their sense of responsibility by trimming an obviously excessive verdict.) Even more clearly, the *Times* Case demonstrated some curious aspects of actual malice by the Alabama legal order, particularly since the state was not the locus of any major publication of the alleged libel. By illustrating the potential power of any legal system in the country to punish and coerce even external publications to restrict their columns to acceptable viewpoints, Alabama virtually forced a readjustment in legal and power relationships.

The press then needs and has obtained judicial protection—a protection that has become more national in scope directly in proportion to and in response to the nationwide expansion of the media. More than that, as we have suggested, the newspaper and magazine industry is well situated to respond to judicial cues and to seek judicial protection. Legal service is quite simply a necessary cost of business in so large-scale an industry, and expert advice in the conduct of day-to-day operations as well as the conduct of litigation is thus readily available. Publishers are prominent people with out-of-the-ordinary political influence, whose endorsement and goodwill are courted. (The *Cleveland Press*, for example, had unquestionably been the single most potent force in choosing the mayor of that city for three decades, while political organizations have been moribund. The *Newark Evening News* successfully prevented any new taxes in New Jersey for a period of a quarter of a century when leaders of both parties conceded its fiscal desirability.) In the case of both appointive and elective judges, newspapers often have both interest and influence.

In conducting litigation, the newspaper industry has the advantage of retained, expert counsel; it is a generally tightly knit industry with citywide cooperation between publications for such purposes as negotiations with unions, quite common in those municipalities that are not one-company towns, and with national organizations that facilitate broader acquaintance and cooperation. It can and does wrap the mantle of free speech about itself. With eager readiness and haughty aplomb, prominent spokesmen for the industry have not been above arguing in court that application of minimum-wage laws or antitrust provisions to newspapers violates freedom of the press. Even publications conspicuously unfriendly to Supreme Court libertarianism assume a vastly different stance when issues touching on their own freedom of expression are concerned. The *Chicago Tribune,* for example, a stalwart critic of the Warren Court, with regular front-page cartoons depicting "mad scientist" judges ruining the country, has been for decades an outstanding advocate in print and court of freedom of the press, appearing at times on behalf of the rights of pamphleteers and other noncommercial publications.

In short, financial and legal power and political influence, both of the personal-elite type, and broad mass-variety coincide with strong symbolic and practical values to bring courts into positive action on behalf of the printed word. The emergence of media as probably the major unifying force in our society has been reflected in their unprecedented and progressive release from external bounds, at least of a legal nature. Certainly, the newspaper today is less answerable in the courts than at any previous time in history; the restraints of conformity are largely the informal pressures involved in satisfying potential readers and advertisers.

The mass-circulation publications are also able to adjust with alacrity to court actions. In one sense, this ability to learn of legal changes and adjust to court nuances increases the control of the legal order. But, basically, the fact that newspapers have the legal talent available as well as the information accessible to precisely adjust verbal behavior allows them to act with relative immunity from trouble on most matters and to gauge the safest approximation to sought behavior when risks are deemed necessary. That is, they can obtain information, more-or-less precise calculations of risks or safe alternative, perhaps indirect wordings that still accomplish the essential aims. The effectiveness of such advice seems confirmed by experience; a New York newspaper found its losses were cut to tiny fractions of previous years after engaging counsel to supervise its daily output. A study of newspaper practices in that city indicated generally the almost certain financial gain of those who paid relatively high sums to skilled attorneys to scan the paper in proof.[14] This is so in spite of the fact that the major cause of libel verdicts is inaccurate reporting rather than a function of overtly actionable language.

In one area—the coverage of crime news and other litigations—courts and media have fairly regularly come into collision. By the 1940s, judicial powers to punish for contempt were severely limited. (An extension of the *New York Times* Case, Garrison *v.* Louisiana involving the now famous District Attorney of New Orleans, established the same limits with respect to use of criminal libel as a substitute for contempt powers.) In recent years extravagant and irresponsible press coverage of trials, in many instances clearly jeopardizing the possibilities of a fair trial, has resulted in a call for greater court control of criminal coverage. It seems evident at this writing that more stringent controls will be employed, but they are unlikely to do little more, and probably less, than limit coverage of the jurors during the trial and check some blazing out-of-court statements and the spread of irresponsible, inadmissible coverage before a public under conditions that can seep into jury consciousness. Post-trial coverage clearly and, most likely, early, pretrial coverage will be inhibited to a most minor extent.

By and large, then, the printed media are well-structured

---

14. M. Marvin Berger, "Detecting Libel Before It Appears," *Editor and Publisher* (May 29, 1937), 7.

to cope with court reactions. The limits imposed on them are relatively small; most libel actions do not revolve around any special opinion of importance, and little of this type of information is held back for legal reasons, especially in contrast to more potent and efficacious socio-economic pressures, which demonstrably often succeeds in postponing immediate coverage and sufficiently often to suggest some significant stories never are covered. On the other hand, the courts are generally allies of media freedom and will react strongly and positively to legal restrictions when contested before them, and the industry is well-situated to bring such matters to a head.

THE REGULATED MEDIA AND THE LEGAL ORDER

Although the news industry finds a major ally in the courts, television and radio have not experienced either significant liberation or restraint as a consequence of court action. Regulated chiefly by federal administrative decisions, the television-radio combines have taken their cues from the Federal Communications Commission and occasionally Congress as to scope of comment, when they have looked to the political system at all. But, in general, they have voluntarily curtailed their social involvement in quest of maximization of financial return and minimization of controversy.

Inherently, the visual-aural media are handicapped in their dealings with news, having only the advantage of immediate communication while being totally handicapped as to the possibility of coverage. (At the time the major networks moved from fifteen-minute to thirty-minute evening news programs, a network circulated a vivid memo showing a fifteen-minute script covered only a few columns of the *New York Times* front page; newspapers were unkind enough to point up the corollary; even a thirty-minute program covered less than a full page.)[15] At the same time, the financial pressures to continue in a solely entertainment vein

15. *New York Times,* September 3, 1963.

are almost irresistible; the FCC indeed has exerted its influence largely to facilitate, even to require, public service
commentary and coverage.

When the courts have overruled the FCC in its conduct
of the industry, it has been largely on matters of property
rights—who should get a station license, effects of competi-
tive licensing and the like, or technological problems, rather
than on content or coverage. When President Johnson was
given time to address the country on the Bay of Tonkin
incident in 1964 without equal time to Senator Goldwater,
the courts gave rather short shrift to the latter's suit.[16] In
general, it is the FCC that sets the standards, and currently
its desire is so strongly to foster public discussion by television, with rather meager success, that complaints about
content are unlikely to be effective. In a few instances—
remarkably few—broadcasting content has been an issue on
renewal of a license or in the granting of a license to a company with an existing situation and therefore a record that
could be judged. Typically, as in the *New York Daily News*
Case or the Pacifica dispute, the FCC has ultimately found
for the licensee and the courts have not been involved. In
1966, however, the United States Court of Appeals in Washington, often the determinative tribunal in administrative
matters, reached a decision that may alter this pattern. The
court ordered the FCC to reconsider its renewal of a television station, taking into account not only its improved
racial coverage under new management since 1964, but also
its previous behavior. Even more significantly, it permitted
public groups, including church groups, to successfully raise
the issue of broadcast practice.[17]

It is, however, doubtful that widespread use of this
power to challenge will ensue. Thus, even the very vulnerable FCC policy of effectively requiring religious broad-

16. *New York Times,* October 22, 1964; October 29, 1964.
17. *Office of Communication of the United Church of Christ, et al* v. *FCC,*
     359 F. 2d., 994 (D.C. Cir., 1966).

casting by stations was not raised in the courts until 1967, by which time the commission effectively forestalled the issue by lumping religious programs with other public-service broadcasts. Although the California ban on pay television was overruled, it was done so on state as well as federal grounds. And although Congressman Adam Clayton Powell fell afoul of the legal order as a result of his "bag woman" remarks on television, libel seldom results from television broadcasts, as only a limited number of programs provide a basis. (Indeed, in most states, television remarks are technically the less serious tort, slander, unless a script is used or the program taped; only gradually are decisions removing this absurd anachronism.)

PUBLISHING AND FILMS: A MIDDLE GROUND

Somewhere in between these two extremes lie the book and movie industries. Their content and potential audiences make them more likely to run afoul of local censors. The primary locus of restraint is in the administrative process rather than the judicial, and the courts are not only in an appellate relationship, but also in a less well-defined and more shifting one than with any of the news media. Significant exercise of judicial power clearly occurs, but by and large the gatekeepers in this domain are the local police, boards of censors, and the like, who must be informed of and to some extent convinced of legal decisions. The facts of life of this filtration, the rather more emotional level of discourse involved here, and perhaps even the less immediate nature of the materials and the structure of the enterprises have made court action less determinative of actual behavior and policies rather more wavering, at least in comparison to the "pure" press enterprises.

Clearly, censorship rather than libel is the chief menace of these quasi-informative, quasi-entertainment media. Only during the past two decades have movies been deemed to be protected by constitutional standards. Paralleling this incorporation of the First Amendment freedoms was a necessary prelude to Supreme Court intervention on matters of censorship of books on obscenity and other grounds. On the state level, too, the notion of applying national constitutional standards to questions of aesthetics and morality is relatively novel. Administrative error or procedural irregularity has been a more common basis for court action.

The need for some modus vivendi, for some principles of administrative deference and accommodation, has seemed evident. Diffusion of enforcement is the pattern, both in the sense that local units are involved and that authority is also divided in the locality. (This is, of course, less true of movies, where there have often been state or city licensing authorities established by law; yet, even under such conditions, the police, prosecutors, and others still have often had overlapping discretion under other statutes.) Thus, the courts are somewhat dependent on the good will of those on the enforcement line, particularly since implementation of judicial standards in the domain of pornography is intrinsically more affected by subjective judgment than many other areas. Further, account must be taken of the mushrooming and sometimes the persistence of local self-appointed watchdogs of morality of the "Watch and Ward" variety. The alternative to local administrative regulation has historically been vigilante operations with little external restraint; those who advocate abandonment of legal standards in this area seem oblivious to this reality.

In essence, too, neither the film industry nor the book industry are as well situated to litigate as newspapers—although they are in much the same position as magazines. They are, to be sure, reasonably large and relatively affluent enterprises and have legal staffs. But the critical point of interaction between legal authorities and the consumer typically involves not the strongholds of the industry, but its weakest links, the local distributors. Even more precisely, it is often the individual theatre or bookseller who is on the firing line, with his motivation to litigate dependent on the reaction and his own perception of the reliability of a distant —usually New York—publisher or film company. The influence of these enterprises is great but diffused, and, consequently, it is usually minor in the locale involved. It may even be advantageous for a publisher to encourage prohibition in one locale to gain notoriety elsewhere; a "banned in Boston" label may be the greatest asset a film or book can have. Outside legal resources may be slow in action and insensitive to the local milieu or unappreciated and discriminated against in some courts.

Films, of course, have been more vulnerable than books. The emotional impact visual material can have has created uneasiness about its unrestrained use, whereas books are more familiar objects whose impact is more readily discounted; the official sanctioning of books in the schools, the subsidization of reading in libraries, and the requirement for reading also help create a situation where people avoid reading. The prevailing attitude is usually that people who could be harmed by books are unlikely to use them. This is less the attitude toward movies, based partly on the fact that the historical audience for the industry is extremely youthful.

The tight control exercised over the cinema—both legal and unofficial—has been radically relaxed in recent years. It is too much to state flatly that legal processes created that liberalization, for profound changes in attitude and action have concomitantly taken place with regard to movies and, indeed, other modes of communication. Not only has there been a distinct alteration of mores with respect to such matters as public expression of sex, but also there has been a diversification of social attitudes well beyond previous experience. With much more profound social disagreement evident, legal processes assume an importance that is more salient, less consistent, yet more strategic. By and large, law in a consensual community enforces what would normally occur anyway; but, in a pronouncedly divided situation, the potency of legal action, in terms of shaping opinion and behavior, is profoundly enhanced.[18]

THE MUNDANE PROBLEM OF DAY-TO-DAY ENFORCEMENT

As we move from relatively well-developed industries into the domain of more spontaneous, less organized expression, the role of courts becomes less systematic; even more, it becomes almost exhortatory—one of hopefully influencing the immediate policy maker to voluntarily comply. Here too, the protections vary, with the printed word most established in its privileges. Over roughly a thirty-year period, the Court has enunciated broad standards to protect the pamphleteer, who by legal precedent cannot be prevented from distribution on the basis of possible littering or failing to identify authors. Public meetings may not be arbitrarily prohibited. All of these and more are outgrowths of standards formerly invoked by state courts prior to this century. Today, they are protected and applied at the federal level and almost uniformly interpreted in terms broader than their former application.

But such legal findings only suggest and hardly begin to prove that freedom exists, for it is in local authorities and their actions in implementation that the impact will be felt. It seems likely that two other phenomena, associated in complex ways with judicial nationalization of law, have contributed to more pervasive implementation of the products of decisions.

The development of truly national communications serves to call attention to the requirements of legality. A community offends national standards of morality—not just legality—at the peril of exposure to the world in the pitiless, remorseless style of modern communications. Such discussion of one's iniquity is difficult to handle, particularly since

18. A study of booksellers by James Levine (Michigan State University; unpublished) indicates less legal action is attempted in restrictive and nonurban environments, apparently because sellers internalize conforming attitudes.

implicit sanctions in loss of external trade, new population, esteem, educational recognition, and the like are all possible results of such attention. During the nineteenth century, the slavery issue and problems associated with class warfare attracted attention; during the twentieth century, beginning perhaps with the Scopes evolution circus trial (where the anti-evolution law was upheld but the penalty invalidated) national attention has developed on abstract issues of self-expression.

The second phenomenon has been the emergence of a network of organizations devoted to support such liberties. The most well-known is, of course, the American Civil Liberties Union, which has acted in many ways as a pyramid or mother organization, sponsoring more specialized structures. Thus enforcement of rights is not left to the isolated individual, but is bolstered both within and without the community. Even local consensus may not always prevent contesting an official action.

The existence of such structures is important in that it makes salient and significant the rights themselves; it imparts a sense of personal significance, social solidarity, and support for potential litigants. This is a deterrent to officials not anxious to pursue a matter in the courts and a source of resources for those forced to persist in a course of legal resistance. It is clear that, in the absence of such group structuring, many civil-liberties matters would be ignored unless of prime concern to the potential litigant or a small number of individuals whose relationship and advantage in the matter were readily perceivable. The existence of organizations not only spreads the cost of such ventures, but also makes the sharing of expenditures a relatively easy process and provides a communications medium for mobilization of attention and resources.[19] Thus, such cases as an individual accused of

19. Mancur Olson, *The Logic of Collective Action* (Cambridge, Mass.: Harvard University Press, 1965) is a provocative treatment of the problem of allocating costs and promoting social action or inaction in an organizational context.

vagrancy or involving a minor fine can be pursued to establish a legal point far beyond the immediate issue at stake.

What happens, though, once the legal principle is established? Assertion of rights by large organizations with manifest legal talent is one thing; individual or casual organizational action another. Action by police in such matters as free speech often involves immediate, on-the-scene decisions. To interrupt a speaker for reasons of crowd safety, to refuse permission to a pamphlet distributor, to stand and pass out materials in a particular locale have immediate consequences. Later vindication by a court cannot have the remedial consequences that alteration of a libel verdict has; certainly, in face-to-face situations, it is often true that "the media constitute the message." To speak at another time or another place involves a different opportunity, not an equivalent one, or perhaps no opportunity at all, the occasion for expression gone, the pace, drama, and momentum of discussion disrupted.

It thus becomes crucial to find the extent to which officials are sensitized to claims of liberty, and, unfortunately, studies of this sort have not been forthcoming. Some indices are available, however.

Although police pay close attention to decisions on criminal procedure, they are seemingly less likely to worry about decisions on liberty generally. The professional journal *Police Chief,* for example, lists literally hundreds of training conferences held every year, but a perusal of three years' topics (1963–1965) show none on problems of the First Amendment. Attention is drawn in this journal and others scrutinized in this study—*Police* and *Police Journal*—to recent court decisions on arrest, search, and interrogation procedure but not to liberty matters. Only in recent years has attention been drawn in police discussion to some aspects of expression as a consequence of civil-rights demonstrations, under the rubric "handling crowds." And when space was devoted to liberty as a topic in a symposium on civil-rights demonstrations, the Bill of Rights was reprinted virtually verbatim, and the rest of the article was a totally uninformative rephrasing of the document.

Only in the more progressive police schools are such topics as freedom of speech touched on, and in cursory fashion. The extent to which such matters are unconsciously ignored and to which error can creep in was indicated in a 1966 report on a New York City examination for police promotion. It was found that points were scored on a crowd protest situation for applications, indicating that, in the event a crowd refused to have a spokesman state grievances, it was to be dispersed—manifestly an illegal procedure.[20] A policeman, in short, who was properly informed on the state of civil liberties was actually penalized for his information. The sum of all such biases in police work is, no doubt, more repressive than any single factor.

Recent years, however, have witnessed obvious changes that will increasingly have effect. Prominent police leaders have progressively been chosen from those who have added to their education, usually a law degree. The increased emphasis on college-trained and sophisticated policemen brings new attitudes to the force. The emergence of special police colleges, with administrators and staffs not exclusively dedicated to providing cookbook programs for day-to-day routine, is even more promising.

A further comparison of these police journals of today with those of a decade previous indicated considerable difference in emphasis. Two recent years of each of those mentioned earlier were compared with their counterparts of ten years previous. Older coverage emphasized crime detection, with occasional forays into such esoteric (and sometimes right-wing) topics as our Asian foreign policy. Today's journals feature discussions of race relations, juvenile treatment, community projects by the police—in short, the sociological

---

20. *New York Times,* January 11, 1967; memo of Seymour Bieber in *Mark et al.* v. *Lang et al.,* January 5, 1967 (unpublished).

setting of police work rather than narrow technology. And two of the journals have had recent articles on the one topic of civil expression most germane to their focus—the right of a policeman to participate in demonstrations, particularly on behalf of equality. As the publications emphasize, this problem has been raised largely because the new breed of policeman has broader interests and is less likely to accept such shibboleths as his "being on duty twenty-four hours a day" than the traditional policeman.

Similarly, it seems clear that local administrators, particularly in large municipalities, have become more cognizant of basic constitutional standards in connection with ministerial functions such as issuing meeting licenses or renting halls. Occasional questions may arise on the fringes of doctrines, or administrators may consciously violate the standard for immediate purposes knowing they will be overruled at a later date, but a consciousness of controlling principles is operative in ways affording considerable latitude to expression.

ACADEMIC FREEDOM: A SPECIAL ADMINISTRATIVE PROBLEM

Some freedoms completely under administrative controls may flourish in the absence of legal remedy, depending on the power relationships involved and the attitude toward freedom of the participants. Thus, academic freedom, the right of teachers and students to discuss openly and freely controversial matters, is relatively secure at most college-level institutions, although it is not enforceable in court, by and large. Even professional tenure—with rare exceptions, as in New York public institutions—is not usually a matter of law or contract, but a moral obligation. What tends to keep administrations in check is their own self-restraint in most instances and the ultimate mobilization of moral and professional censure, with the threat of lower prestige and inferior faculties and potentially, therefore, decreased revenue. Nonetheless, it must be noted that recourse for an individual faculty member is seldom really available either in court or out should violations of his freedom occur. A censure by the American Association of University Professors may bring ultimate apologies—and sometimes a payment of some compensation—years after the damage is done. Until recently, the rights of students were even less protected, with both courts and internal university structures accepting the "substitute parent" notion that administrations acted solely for the good of the student and therefore needed no limitations. In recent years, some universities have been developing internal procedures for due process protection of students, and courts have increasingly been willing to hear cases where obvious abuse of discretion has occurred. In 1967, Judge Constance Baker Motley of New York held that public school students had a right to be represented by an attorney where serious disciplinary action, such as expulsion, was threatened. How far such attitudes will extend—both in a geographic sense and with regard to type of issues covered—is difficult to foresee.

THE OUTER LIMITS OF COURT CONTROL

In general, as academia suggests, the courts define the rights of expression of institutions or the press but are more likely to define intrainstitutional freedom as a matter of contract, the interpretation of agreement, or a question of ownership rather than of civil liberties. The law defines the rights of the press as an institution but has almost nothing to say about the power of the individual reporter or editor. Even the columnist whose writings are refused publication in the face of his contract can expect only money damages and cannot compel publication. By and large, an employer can exact as much verbal conformity of his employees as the market, possible adverse publicity, and the personalities of both permit. The courts, as a rule, will not intervene even in a patently vicious firing. Similarly—and more justifiably

—arguments on church doctrine, political ideology, and family loyalty are all questions left to the participants. Wherever possible, certain kinds of problems are avoided by the incumbents of the law jobs in deference to the difficulty of dealing with them constructively or because of the power of the participants.

Where evaluatory procedures of affective relationships are the heart of the matter, the legal order is especially reluctant to intervene, for court processes can only operate in an inefficient or provocative manner. A former employer can say things in a letter of evaluation that would produce a substantial verdict otherwise, and literary critics have license that is almost unbounded. (We have already noted that it was through analogizing public officials to employees or artists offering their creations to the public that judges extended the right of popular criticism of governmental officials.) Similarly, credit ratings are privileged, although they may drastically affect an individual's opportunities.

However, the federal government now intervenes regularly in one area of employer–employee comment, where it concerns not individuals per se, but union–management relations. Comments by union officials or membership about the employer, individual or corporation, may be an unfair labor practice (particularly if made by picketing or public presentation). Similarly, what the employer says about the union may be of governmental concern, and his actions and statements about individual workers, even with regard to their competence as workers, may be controlled or punished if the ultimate purpose or effect is to control or discourage unionization. The Wagner and Taft-Hartley Acts, in short, changed the relationship of employer and employee even with regard to matters of expression.

The government, too, has been forced to recognize an alteration of its role with its own employees and accept court intervention where none was formerly forthcoming. Although government officials have "absolute privilege" in connection with their duties, including comment upon employees (which was in fact the issue in Barr *v.* Matteo), punishment, including dismissal, is now conditioned by due process requirements.

To the present time, however, surveillance of employees, including intrabuilding electronic eavesdropping, has been outside court control. Even where clearly illegal, as in wiretapping, there has been little legal punishment. The extent of such practices has not been obvious, and perhaps fortunately so, for realization would probably inhibit expression. The major efforts of eavesdroppers appear to have been in the exciting and burgeoning field of industrial espionage —one company against another—so that there is both a minimum of danger to freedom and a maximum possibility of countermeasures. But surveillance and eavesdropping is a function of relationships between employer and employee and seems likely to be resolved more as a consequence of union bargaining and control than as a societal measure. Even governmental snooping on employees has been brought under some scrutiny not by legal process, but by political means, through congressional committee investigations. Since there are fads and fashions in congressional concerns, it is possible to be skeptical of overall and continuous accomplishment.

To a large extent, the courts have failed to establish any protection from nongovernmental intrusion into private life, and they inhibit government from such intrusion only to the extent of preventing government from inflicting direct harm or punishment. Thus, the authorities are prevented from firing employees or prosecuting individuals on the basis of evidence secured from such intrusions. But it has proven difficult to enunciate legal doctrines and controls to eliminate the intrusions. The consequences of public revelations are seemingly uncontrollable without severe consequences to public informational processes. Private intrusions on privacy are in fact difficult to detect, require elaborate means to fight, and establish few principles of law. The best opportunity for future liberty may well be the creation of governmental structures (or better yet, voluntary organizations analogous to the American Civil Liberties Union or a shift in interest of that group itself) to vindicate the rights of the individual not merely as against government, but also as against the intrusions of other people and other institutions.

By and large, it is also beyond the scope of the courts generally to intervene in positive affirmations by governmental units. Curriculum, required courses, and expenditure of funds for specific types of educational programs, represent one facet beyond court action. Another—and these examples hardly exhaust the range but merely illustrate it— is the power of government to generate its own point of view. Congress has at times rather vainly attempted to stem the tide of publicity emanating from the executive; the courts have no such responsibility and little control—to their relief and ours. Expenditures to educate, to shape opinion, and to recruit opinion are indeed political questions and are left to political processes.

Indeed, the very paucity of court power to thwart such expression, the total absence of any right to become a Pure Food and Drug Administration, is perhaps the finest and fullest justification of such authority as it claims. Even in weakness there is sometimes strength.

6

The Court and the Public

It is altogether appropriate that both the opening and closing chapters of this book should be concerned with the relationship of the Supreme Court and public opinion. That relationship is indeed the alpha and omega of the nature of the Court, partaking both of the problems in democratic theory broached in Chapter 1 and the more practical operative considerations dealt with here.

To some, the relationship is simple. Indeed, there are those to whom such a relationship is apparently improper or nonexistent. Certainly, that would be the contention with regard to the influence of the populace on the Court. Thus legal fundamentalists long insisted that only judgment was being brought to bear on cases and that temporal conditions and influences were irrelevant. Fred Rodell, with his suggestion that the Court follows the election returns "of ten or twelve years before,"[1] implies that little happens once a Justice comes to the Court, that he persists in deciding matters in the light of his fundamental attitudes. This, too, has been the increasing perspective of Schubert and others among the leading behaviorist political scientists focusing on judicial attitudes. (Still others in their camp have taken a more tentative view.)

It has also been possible to see the effect side of the equation as equally uncomplicated. Again, the legal fundamentalist was basically indifferent to popular reaction to Court decisions, regarding any reaction except obedience as improper and uncalled for; the Court had spoken, and that was the end of it. Popular reaction led to civil wars or displays of petulance. Even sophisticated legalists believed that the Court difficulties with majoritarian impulses could be avoided by proper channeling of judicial power through a correct understanding of the *legal* limits of Court power. For example, Charles Warren's *The Supreme Court in United States History* is a multi-volume chronology of popular rebelliousness, viewed by the author somewhat resignedly, somewhat reprovingly, much as one regards youthful hyperactivity or a case of puppy love, modified by a very few admissions on rare occasions that the Court may have overreached itself and precipitated some of its own difficulties.

Other writers, however, have understood the matter in more complex terms. Charles Evans Hughes, for example, suggested that the Supreme Court could have avoided conflict by avoidance of legally doubtful decisions where public opinion was surcharged with emotion. He thus acknowledged the relevance both of popular attitude toward Court decision and its reciprocal consequences.[2]

---

1. Rodell, p. 9.
2. Charles Evans Hughes, *The Supreme Court of the United States* (Garden City, N.Y.: Garden City Publishing Co., 1936).

Empirical evidence seems to support more complex notions of the relationship of mass opinion and judicial opinions. Virtually all the Justices supported the anti-Japanese measures during World War II, but some of the same individuals stood fast during the hue and cry of the McCarthy period. Stronger evidence on the effect side of the ledger can be adduced; thus, Court action appears to have been instrumental in changing and aggregating attitudes toward apportionment, segregation, and prayer in the schools, but it has had a harder time of it with regard to securing a consensus on proper police methods and seems to have no visible effect on popular attitudes as to, say, antitrust policy. To depart from Supreme Court evidence, it is noteworthy that a study by Cohen and others of popular attitudes on the question of parent–child relationships, shows practically no relationship between legal decisions based on common-law practices and what people regard as proper and desirable.[3] Nor has there been any appreciable change in the law to accommodate shifting opinion, which is strikingly divergent from legal norms, being both more and less severe in different areas of such relationships.

The effort here is to attempt to delineate the conditions under which legal influence is at a maximum and a minimum. We will then turn that analysis directly to bear on Supreme Court–public opinion relationships.

FACTORS AFFECTING THE COURT'S INFLUENCE

SALIENCY

Generally, before a decision can alter opinion, it must be widely noticed. (Oddly, this is not an absolute necessity; by indirectly altering behavior, changes in attitudes may be induced. In this case, only the potential enforcers of a de-

---

3. Julius Cohen et. al., *Parental Authority* (New Brunswick, N.J.: Rutgers University Press, 1958).

cision need be aware of it. However, the process would in most instances be so slow that it would be difficult to speak of cause even in loose terms.) This need is analogous to the traditional story of the muletender who always spoke quietly to his animals but hit them on the head with a two-by-four "to attract their attention."

Why a decision does or does not attract popular reaction is itself a problem of no mean dimensions. Certainly, the mass media play a large role, and their perceptions of what the public wants particularly affects what the public gets. Significant cases socially and legally may attract attention. The Steel Seizure Case was widely reported, as befitted a case pitting big labor against giant industry, with assertions of presidential prerogative and questions of the war and emergency powers of the national government. But the Flag Salute Cases, involving relatively narrow constitutional questions, attracted concern partly because of their unique timing—the period immediately after the fall of France and our own entry into World War II—and partly because of the sheer human drama of little children waging a battle for religious conviction as against an indifferent but relentless bureaucratic intolerance. The Scopes trial was surely one of the least significant legal battles of all times, but, because of its protagonists and the drama of their confrontation, it has provided the raw material for books, dramas, movies, and even scholarly analysis. Of course, salience is necessary to secure compliance with or acceptance of a decision; it may also provoke opposition. The Dred Scott Case was well-known indeed to the Abolitionists!

CONGRUENCY WITH ESTABLISHED VALUES

On the whole, most people—or, at least, American people—do not ideologize, but develop a series of relatively discrete attitudes toward specific matters that intrude themselves on their consciousness. When these attitudes conflict, it is usual to disguise, rationalize, or avoid confrontation if at all possible. Where confrontation is inevitable, alteration of attitudes takes place. One or both elements are displaced or a new synthesis emerges.

Court decisions almost invariably involve a confrontation of values, sometimes embodied in the facts themselves. Such confrontations also take place in other aspects of political life, but by and large the results emerge solely as "thumbs up" or "thumbs down" decisions. Court opinions, however, involve a process of ratiocinations in which the confrontation is often directly asserted and discussed. Where a higher-level value—or one more deeply and emotionally held—is involved, such discussion may well result in abandonment of an immediate gain for a longer-term interest. Although the President occasionally presents similar considerations in speeches or press conferences and, indeed, has the advantage of continuous response and discussion when he chooses to employ them, the Court is characterized by its need to conduct such a discourse and its thoroughness in these matters.

PATTERN OF SUPPORT AND OPPOSITION

The appearance of support or opposition has significant consequences in both activating latent opinion and in converting mugwumps to one position or the other. In this respect, the most significant sources of support are usually the President and Congress. It is likely that President Eisenhower's long-time equivocal stand on desegregation hurt the development of a national consensus, whereas President Kennedy's unqualified endorsement of the school prayer decision helped achieve tenuous agreement. (Indeed Kennedy's pithy remark suggesting that more sincere prayers could be evoked without limit in homes and places of worship helped define the meaning of a badly reported decision.) The emergence or lack of broad-scale support can also be determinative. In the school prayer decisions, the fact that virtually all religious groups came to accept the decision helped defeat strongly backed moves to secure constitutional amendments introduced by Senator Everett Dirksen to satisfy "the prayer-throb of the American people." The opposition was symbolized by the appearance of Father Robert Drinan, a leading Catholic scholar on constitutional law, who asked rhetorically whether it was likely that the Senators proposing the amendment truly were more protective of religion than the spokesmen of all major faiths. Earlier, too, the amendment suffered an important symbolic loss when its original sponsor, Congressman Frank Backer, became convinced the effort was in error and withdrew his support.

Support patterns may follow along interest-group lines or institutional patterns. Thus, Alan Westin concluded that the Supreme Court decisions were overturned by Congress in those instances in which the business community lined up with other groups for a broad, general anti-Court approach.[4]

Similarly, regional or geographic factors may play a role. Because opposition to the original desegregation decisions was regionally compact, official opposition was more unequivocal and violent than might have occurred had the same numbers been more uniformly dispersed. (Even these, precipitating actions by the leadership in Virginia, which by sociological indices should have been moderate in its policies, stiffened attitudes in the South, leading to massive resistance.) At the same time, latent regional hostilities and displacement of guilt may have helped precipitate the otherwise national consensus for civil rights. Recognition that further social changes would have to be implemented throughout the country may have helped dampen some of the ardor. Analogously, the school prayer and religious education decisions tend to be followed in the pluralistic, cosmopolitan metropolitan regions and are more likely to be ignored in homogeneous rural school districts. On the whole, this leads to a relatively desirable equilibrium, since the

---

4. Alan Westin, "Corporate Appeals to Congress for Relief from Supreme Court Rulings," paper read before the American Political Science Convention, September, 1962.

effects of coercion are thus kept to a minimum precisely where they would be greatest and most capable of producing discord.[5]

THE SPECIFIC DECISION AND THE DECISION CONTEXT

In studying voting choices, social scientists have developed the concept "cross-pressures"; the impact of conflicting influences is seen as relatively immobilizing. The Court is at its most fortunate if it can secure widespread support for each and every decision. Since, practically speaking, that is an impossible program—on the average, about half of its litigants are going to be disappointed—it must rely on more generalized support patterns. What it must do or have done for it is to convince those disagreeing with a substantive decision that acceptance is somehow consistent with their overall self-interest. This can be done, where all else fails, by appeal to the need for preservation of the social fabric itself, the ultimate necessity for power of decision roosting somewhere. This Hobbesian appeal—"pray for the the welfare of the government, for if it were not for its existence men would swallow one another up alive"—is perhaps a reasonable one but often sounds remote. In the guerrilla-war stage of opposition to the segregation decision in the South, it was reasonable to appeal to law and order as a slogan. On the whole, this is remote and illogical in, say, a stranger-picketing case where only five protesters are involved. However, some elements of the decision may well promise success for the union in other cases. Alternatively, attack on the Court may destroy or weaken judicial review of administrative decisions, which may not loom as desirable. To the extent that interests intertwine, and it is perceived that that is so, the consequences of unfavorable decisions are minimized. It would be foolhardy, for example, for civil-rights groups to turn on the Court as a consequence of a single decision. The very

---

5. For a fuller treatment of these points see Samuel Krislov, *The Supreme Court in the Political Process,* Chap. 6.

form and substance of legal decisions tend to emphasize the interrelatedness of results, the existence of widespread and crosscutting ramifications of Court decisions.

The Court also has the advantage of presenting its decisions in a form emphasizing continuity and interrelatedness of previous results, suggesting that inevitability of its actions and giving notice of what is likely to occur, therefore easing the shock of what in fact is decided. Thus, although the pace of the apportionment decisions and their ultimate severity were not predictable, the direction seemed clear once the Court arrived at the decision in Gomillion v. Lightfoot (1960), much as the white primary was foredoomed by United States v. Classic, which had nothing to do with racial voting.

The acceptance or rejection of a decision, indeed its impact generally, may be related to its general timing. Thus, the conviction of stockbroker Richard Whitney at the height of the depression was seen as confirming the depravity of stock dealers, generally blamed for unfortunate decisions, and its embodiment in the general context of events contributed to far-reaching regulation of securities. On the other hand, the objectively more damaging revelations of collusive, near-fraudulent pricing of electrical supplies by major companies, regarded as among the most responsible in American industry, came at a time when business prestige was at a maximum and had relatively little enduring influence.

THE COSTS OF OPPOSITION
AND THE PENALTIES OF DECISION

It is axiomatic that the opposition to a decision must occur only when the psychic costs of compliance exceed what Chester Barnard called "the zone of indifference," a combination of the tendency to accept authority added to the costs of opposition. Once opposition has occurred with regard to one issue, it is likely that the psychic disposition to obey in other matters will be diminished. The pattern of adherence to Supreme Court decisions is, after all, relatively well-established over decades. If Andrew Jackson really *said* "John Marshall has made his decision; now let him enforce it"—and that is doubtful—Harry Truman certainly *showed* the way to acceptance with his obedience of the Court decision in the Steel Seizure Case. If Governors Faubus and Barnett did manage to put up more than a show of resistance to desegregation, their ultimate acceptance of federal power remains the basic reality, the moral one can deduce from the story.

We know too little about the type of punishment in relation to control of behavior to begin to speculate about the further complication of how conforming behavior leads to approving opinion. Severity of punishment is only one of the factors discouraging violation and opposition; certainty of punishment looms as another factor, and some offenses flourish even when both definite and draconic punishment is involved. Nor does the frequency have to be great; thus, Ralph Brown of Yale Law School concludes that, at the height of the anti-Communist security scare, only 11,500 persons were actually discharged from government or suffered equivalent punishment during the years 1948–1953. Beyond doubt, some of this relatively small number—representing 1/7,560 of employees—were actually security risks on any reasonable criteria.[6] Yet the feeling was widely conveyed that anyone was vulnerable and that virtually everyone was subject to such treatment. A truly systematic account of how this attitude permeated the public service has not yet been written. Yet, such preludes as Brown's volume and studies such as Adam Yarmolinsky's and that of Jahoda and Cook offer some clues. The number suffering official punishment was small, but the number of those involved in preliminary investigations was considerably larger—forty-two times as

---

6. Ralph Brown, Jr., *Loyalty and Security* (New Haven, Conn.: Yale University Press, 1958), pp. 182, 487–8, and 55.

many faced derogatory information.[7] By any standards, it must be concluded that those who were exonerated suffered about as much as those discharged; after trying legal proceedings, they seldom found that exoneration lifted all doubts from over their heads. This essential arbitrariness was coupled with some unbelievably stupid conduct on the part of security boards—like most governmental agencies varying widely in competence and a sense of human dignity, both truly necessary in a presentment of a democratic government in its relationship as employer, as a controller of a man's career, and perhaps his destiny.

How, then, did it end? The short answer is that it was as a consequence of a relaxation in the tensions of the cold war. Yet, although there probably is a basic truth to this, it must be noted that we have faced even the hostilities of Viet Nam with probably greater equanimity and internal tolerance than in any comparable period in our history. Even the fact that in fantasy we can hardly be seen as domestically menaced by our actual opponents does not gainsay the strides in maturity and domestic self-confidence exhibited by our society.

More complex factors ended McCarthyism, both in its exact sense and in broader terms. The reflexive need of a Republican administration to defend the adequacy of its security measures brought it into collision with the exposure efforts of the Senator from Wisconsin. The demonstration of the invalidity, in some cases merely wild exaggeration, of charges brought against most of those involved in sensational stories left only a tiny core of sustained charges of espionage and only a slightly larger record of arguably un-American collaboration of a lesser sort.

All of the elaborated record of past misdeeds truly paled into insignificance in contrast with the demonstrated record of damage being done to contemporary society. Efficiency of

7.   Brown, pp. 55–6. See also Anthony Lewis, "Security: Interim Reports," *The Reporter* September 8, 1955), p. 27; and Marie Jahoda and Stuart W. Cook, "Security Measures and Freedom of Thought," *Yale Law Journal,* LXI (1952), 295.

normal governmental processes was drastically impaired, and agencies involved in cold war activities, for example, the Voice of America, were thoroughly demoralized. Recruitment became a serious problem for defense efforts, especially after the Oppenheimer cause célèbre. When the most prominent scientist associated with public service was publicly disgraced largely on evidence of behavior known to officials before his services were used and after he had disagreed with a new line of policy, government service loomed as something to avoid unless one were not only always discreet and conforming, but also always correct in one's advocacy of policies. (A very few years later, President Kennedy's administration—and that of President Johnson—sought to minimize the damage by awarding Oppenheimer the Enrico Fermi Prize.) As it was demonstrated and gradually accepted that the chief race between the United States and USSR was in scientific achievement rather than between our achievement and their spying, emphasis shifted to the conditions under which we would achieve the most. A freer atmosphere was a requisite both for obtaining the services of quality personnel and using them effectively once employed.

From the standpoint of our topic, the effect on free expression in the society was great indeed, and these evils, too, produced antibodies. Specific individuals in the entertainment and information fields were blacklisted not only as performers, with consequences mainly for themselves and the general atmosphere of repression, but more significantly as writers. Some authors escaped into pseudonyms, other left the country and wrote abroad, and still others ceased to be writers. This engendered some sympathy and created situations demonstrating the excesses of the times—for example, the inability of some of the blacklisted artists to come forward to receive Academy Awards for movie work.

A careful study of academic reactions was undertaken by Lazersfeld and Thielens. They found that, on the whole, very few academics were actually and overtly touched by any specific incidents. Nonetheless, apprehension was common; in most cases, however, the social science professors in their sample reported speaking out *more positively* on relevant public matters than they would have otherwise.[8] (This is difficult to interpret, as it could either represent reality or a distortion. The academic posture has been, in one sense, to build up and magnify the pressures of those years and their consequences; on the other hand, professors would hate to admit personal lack of hardihood and candor with their students, particularly in the face of merely generalized fears.) Since Senator McCarthy virtually took the position that universities were subversive, he united the academic community as it almost never has been before or since. Nevertheless, it was clear from the Lazersfeld-Thielens study that professors of lesser eminence at small schools and with lower-rank salary and security were more vulnerable to pressures to abstain from discussing an issue or inviting a controversial speaker or requiring reading of a book that might be called questionable. In a tentative supplementary statement to their book, they have also suggested that the attitude of the local newspaper toward controversy might well have been a critical determinant of nonconforming behavior, since the local paper could and often did zero in with scorn or support on anyone in the community labeled as suspect, whether the initial attack came nationally or locally. That is to say, national media seldom deal with individuals on a repeated basis; local papers operate on a "names make news" philosophy and therefore were crucial to the individual.

What was the role of the Court in all this? At first, it generally acquiesced, in fact giving the political branches of government the scope to unilaterally define the Communist problem and means of dealing with it. As in ACA *v.* Douds and the Dennis Case, however, acquiescence was expressed with misgivings by the majority and protests by the dissenters. As excesses developed in individual cases, they were limited by

---

8. Paul Lazersfeld and Wagner Thielens, *The Academic Mind* (New York: The Free Press, 1958).

the courts. The vague conspiracy charges in the Lattimore Case were ruled incapable of justifying a criminal trial; in the Peters Case, administrators were held bound by their own announced rules in proceedings of their own making. Even in the earliest stages, the opinions of dissenting judges served as rallying cries for civil libertarians; fairly frequently, they were quoted by Communist groups as vindication. As the Court began to articulate a philosophy of fair dealing with governmental employees, especially in nonsensitive positions, they also in effect restated a minimum of operative respect required toward the sovereign citizen. By the time of the Yates decision, the Justices were willing to directly state that minimum. Finally, through a series of technical decisions that took over a decade, the Court gradually ended the threats of outlawry of the Communist Party.

It can be seen that the courts did not act with drama or abrupt heroism, but in the time-honored legalistic manner, or narrow, almost naïve-seeming thwarting of political excesses along the general line of tactics advocated by Learned Hand. (See Chap. 1.) Even when using the more comprehensive power afforded by judicial review, the Court has tended to minimize the effect, preferring accretive improvement to wholesale confrontation, the "inevitability of gradualness" to inevitable conflict with President and Congress.

It is therefore difficult to say that any concrete result is attributable to the Court itself. Indeed, since we live only in the world as it has actually been experienced, lacking the ability to relive the past with experimentally induced variations, it is even difficult to affirm that the pattern of freedom that prevails today would have been appreciably disturbed had the Court not so acted. The causes of change already discussed, when coupled with demographic change and the emergence of a younger, more educated citizenry, might well account for the emergence of a more enlightened, more tolerant nation of the 1960s from the frightened, tighter society of the 1950s. Court action tended to be in advance of political acceptance of standards of liberty, it is clear, as witnessed by the near success of anti-Court actions in Congress.[9] Yet, the Justices were seldom so daring as to go beyond the approval of the executive branch and therefore perhaps followed rather than preceded public opinion.

It seems likely, however, that more credit must be accorded to Justices. Friend and foe seem to place them in the forefront of the battle, and skirmishes won are the basis of more dramatic victories. We are told that, in Hitler's Europe, the mere raising of moral questions by the Danes and Norwegians changed the personal convictions of the Nazi enforcers themselves, as would be suggested by such social psychological experiments as those of Sherif and Asch.[10] It would appear, therefore, that the substantive advances achieved by the Court would not automatically have been achieved elsewhere in government. (After all, if the Presidency had been not merely willing to accept Court decisions on loyalty programs and security prosecutions, but even determined to achieve the same results as the decisions, no cases would ever have arisen.) We may also speculate that the moral authority of the Court contributed to other political decisions, with perhaps even a "multiplier effect" involved.

THE COURT AND PUBLIC OPINION: ELITE AND MASS SUPPORT

The relationship of the Court to public opinion in relation to free expression presents not one but three major issues: support for the Court itself, support for freedom of expression itself, and the dynamic interplay of these support

---

9. See C. Herman Pritchett, *Congress Versus The Supreme Court* (Minneapolis: University of Minnesota Press, 1961).

10. See Hannah Arendt, *Eichmann in Jerusalem: A Report on the Banality of Evil* (New York: The Viking Press, 1963); Muzafer and Carolyn Sherif, *An Outline of Social Psychology* (New York: Harper & Row, 1956).

patterns. The latter is clearly neither an additive nor subtractive product of the other two, but rather a complex vector of slightly but significantly different patterns.

Support for Court legitimacy is historically based and battle tested. Roosevelt's failure to pack the Court immediately after his smashing 1936 victory, with a majority of the country clearly supporting his substantive aims, looms as the most visible historical vindication. Alone among presidential candidates, Barry Goldwater chose to make the Court a campaign issue, as both Roosevelts did by indirection only—a further tribute to popular support of the Court. Empirical evidence, although meager, bears out the assumption that the populace retains respect and even awe for the Court— "Impeach Earl Warren" signs notwithstanding—and in a manner different from other branches of government. The sketchy evidence to this effect that can be gleaned from Gallup, Roper and NORC polls will be both tested and treated systematically by the Tanenhaus-Murphy study now underway by the Survey Research Center's consortium and enriched by valuable comparisons with attitudes in foreign countries. (Conversations with Professor Tanenhaus indicate that findings will show less prestige is accorded Justices than such categories as "famous scientist." It is impossible to tell whether this new finding is a consequence of more sophisticated questioning or represents a decline in Court prestige.)

Support patterns for substantive decisions of the Court in the freedom of expression is, of course, more variegated depending on concrete issues; like generalized approval of the Court, support varies in time as well. We have already commented on numerous studies tending to confirm the subtlety of the concept of toleration of dissent and the fundamental distrust of liberty, studies sufficiently similar in their findings to suggest to more than one writer that, if the American populace were to vote on the Bill of Rights today, it would be overwhelmingly rejected (see Chap. 1). Of course, such a question will never be tested and, in a certain, sense never can be. The Bill of Rights would, if rejected by this nation, be repealed by amendment or obviously breached with prevailing consent, both of which courses would require extraordinary support or strong intensity of demand. Our liberties have the moral advantage of being written in parchment and were written in parchment precisely to gain moral advantage. The issue cannot be raised *de novo* in any event.

It is fallacious to assume that off-the-cuff responses are necessarily representative of the motive forces we can expect to be evident in a real-life political confrontation. What enlightened discussion, the influences of political leaders, and the mass media will do to channel latent notions is not ascertainable from the relatively casual paper-and-pencil situation of polling. This is particularly crucial when, as noted, these same studies show generalized and stereotyped responses in favor of liberty of expression. Under these circumstances, we have argued both in this chapter and in Chapter 1, the confrontation of conflicting values, albeit on different levels of abstraction, can be a lever for moving attitudes in one direction or another.[11]

This does not, however, mean that these studies are of no moment; on the contrary, they do represent something real, both in the present and in potential at all times, a genuine force to reckon with. It is, therefore, worthwhile to summarize some of the findings.

In general, youth and education are highly correlated with pro-civil-rights attitudes. The West and the East are most libertarian, the South, least. Contradictory findings are reported with respect to party identification and libertarian attitudes. It seems likely that, in the gross, the Republicans may well be more sympathetic because of the educational distribution of the party. It seems, however, clear that controlling for education gives an entirely different picture.

---

11. See the discussions in Shel Feldman (ed.), *Cognitive Consistency* (New York: Academic Press, 1966) and the references therein, especially to the work of Festinger and Abelson.

Active Democrats, in particular, are more likely to be libertarian than their Republican counterparts. It would appear that, in recent years, there has been growing support for libertarian positions, although this sentiment may have recently peaked.[12]

The strong correlations between youth and toleration, as well as educational level and libertarianism, presumably bode well for the next decade or so, as both these correlates can be expected to increase dramatically during that period. Offsetting this, perhaps, are studies indicating more instability of political attitudes among the young and some indications of the politically unfavorable consequences of over-rapid mobility. The repeated shouting down of speakers on college campuses and other well-publicized activities of student activists in recent years have not always suggested a devotion to the principles of civil liberties.

In assessing the dynamic impact of Court and liberty together, the findings of John Kessel in a study of Republicans and conservatives are suggestive and perhaps generalizable.[13] Essentially, he found opposition to both the Court and pro-civil-liberties decisions; but opposition tended to be negatively correlated with information. Those who really understood, even in general terms, what the Court had done overwhelmingly supported it *and* its decisions. Those who were critical tended to be ill-informed, both substantively and in terms of the Court's place in American government. (This dichotomy also tends to be evident in the *National Review* and other organs of conservative intellectualism; conservatives who understand the Court—like Brent Bozell—essentially take sideswipes at it; hammer-and-tongs attacks come from inepts like Rosalie Gordon.[14] This, then, constitutes a

---

12. See also the discussion and references in Chapter 1.
13. John Kessel, "Public Perceptions of the Supreme Court," *Midwest Journal of Political Science*, X (May, 1966), 167.
14. See her absurd *Nine Men Against America* (New Rochelle: America's Future Inc., 1957); but compare with Bozell's writings on the Court.

fatal flaw, at least under present conditions. The opposition must channel its own expression through a leadership that disagrees to a greater or lesser degree with criticism of the Court or the particular decisions. So, when the chips were down, even the highly conservative American Bar Association found it necessary to speak up on behalf of the Court, and others, disapproving of social policy and criminal decisions, must still applaud the freedom of expression opinions. A leadership of several minds on these matters tends to be a weakened one.

A study of national opinion by William Daniels based on the 1964 Survey Research Center presidential-election survey does not seriously alter this picture. Daniels finds the more educated more likely to be critical of the Court, but these are individuals with a low sense of political efficacy and are less likely to have read widely on politics. Further, professionals are less critical of the Court than other groups of comparable socio-economic status. (This is crucial because of the significant role of attorneys in such matters.) Those critical of the Court, however, are more politically active, according to Daniels, and the amount of criticism is much greater nationally than found by Kessel in Seattle. (In view of prevailing southern attitudes, this is not too surprising, but the extent of criticism among those having an expressed attitude is strong. It must be noted that Goldwater made criticism of the Court an express issue, whereas Johnson left the defense somewhat muted.) In general, however, the nominally neutral, generally pro-Court orientation of the populace seems confirmed by the Survey Research data as well.[15]

To a large extent, then, the Court's position and the

---

15. William J. Daniels, "Public Attitudes Toward the United States Supreme Court," paper presented at the Midwest Conference of Political Scientists, April, 1967. A close reading of the data assembled by Daniels suggests that greater refinement of "elite groups" and "mass opinion" is both necessary and possible with respect to the Court as well as other phenomena. Presumably, the Murphy-Tanenhaus study will have major consequences in our knowledge on this matter.

efforts of the civil-liberties organizations tend to depend on elite groups, broadly defined. With rather strong support from leadership groups in society, it is hoped for a reasonable majority from the populace as a whole. Basically, the Court itself has little access to any but elite opinion, and, although it has given consideration to dramatic shifting of methods to gain more popular support, the Justices have been reluctant to experiment with methods that force them to exchange the posture of judicial reticence for problematic gains in popular support; the present two-step flow of opinion seems the most efficient. The Court has abandoned the notion of a single decision day to allow less harried and more thorough press coverage of its actions. Individual Justices—most notably Clark, who, as a prominent dissenter in many decisions, was especially effective—have been freer than was formerly the practice in publicly defending decisions. In the main, however, the Justices have eschewed such suggested innovations as annual messages to Congress or press releases designed to carry their appeal to the populace. They assume, apparently, that the methods of the past by and large have proven effective. As to their new role, now several decades old, of defending in activist manner freedom of expression, they seem severely confident that, in ultimate terms, these values are sufficiently universal in their appeal to overcome the necessary misunderstandings in initial reaction. Ultimately, the Justices must hope that in a real confrontation, with clarification of costs and alternatives, people are basically libertarian.

THE VIRTUE OF THE COURT'S DEFECTS

Some years ago, Professor Harold Berman of the Harvard Law School taught a course in American law at Moscow University. To illustrate his points, he had the students read the text of the Dennis Case and other decisions sustaining the outlawing of the American Communist Party. There was

little objection to this at first, with the students indeed en-
joying and quoting the dissenting opinions of Justices Black
and Douglas to support their disagreement with the official
United States internal policy. Gradually, however, they
realized, as Berman had intended them to, how remote from
their system and how subversive of their familiar methods
such dissents were.[16] The official routine printing of discussion and disagreement, rather than mere anouncement of
majority policy and conclusions, captures in its essence the
difference between a constitutional order and a frozen,
tightly knit regime.

The Court by its very being is a ratiocinating body, one
"which considers before it decides." Its very processes emphasize and incorporate free discussion and respect for the force
of ideas rather than numbers. Political forces make themselves felt in terms of votes, on the Court as well as off; it is
well that Court action has proven to be more a matter of providing mitigating restraints than steering courses and setting
policy. Even in the field of defining the modes and content
of free expression, utlimate reliance must be on the political
system and populace as a whole rather than "a bevy of platonic guardians." But, as a part of the system as a whole, the
Court is as uniquely fitted to articulate the values of expression as it is to defend them. It has found in political expression a social interest, a clientele group worthy both of itself
and, even more significantly, of our society.

---

16. *New York Times,* February 16, 1963; April 14, 1963.

A Note on Further Reading

The full texts of Supreme Court decisions are reported in *United States Reports* (U.S.), the official publication printed by the government; *The Supreme Court Reporter* (S.Ct.), which provides a digest and indexing system; and the *Lawyers' Edition* (L.Ed.), which—in addition to text, digest, and indexing system—contains notes on many of the leading cases analyzing the decision in terms of its precedents. The Table of Cases gives all three references for each case cited in the main portion of this volume. If the student has a law library available to him, he will discover all three series. Most college and public libraries acquire only one. The two nonofficial series provide considerably more analytical paraphernalia, particularly for linking one decision with others on the same subject, but all three contain exactly the same text.

The issue of free speech commands frequent reassessment. The casebook by William B. Lockhart, Yale Kamisar, and Jesse H. Choper, *The American Constitution* (St. Paul:

West Publishing Co., 1967) is probably the one which reflects the most concern with up-to-the-minute issues in this area. The annual surveys by the *Harvard Law Review*, articles in the *Supreme Court Annual* (University of Chicago Press) and the yearly mimeographed analysis of the American Jewish Congress are most helpful in this respect.

Historical analysis has been treated in the early pages of this book. The most scholarly work remains Levy's important *Legacy of Suppression: Freedom of Speech and Press in Early American History**[1] (New York: Harper Torchbooks, 1963), although it should be read carefully in conjunction with Henry Schofield's essay "Freedom of the Press in the United States" (*Papers and Proceedings of the American Sociological Society* [1915], pp. 67–116) and Zachariah Chafee's *Freedom of Speech* (New York: Harcourt, Brace and Howe, 1920) which it purports to demolish but actually modifies only slightly. John Roche's essay "American Liberty" in Konvitz and Rossiter, *Aspects of Liberty* (Ithaca: Cornell University Press, 1958) is also useful. Edward Dumbauld's *The Bill of Rights* (Norman: University of Oklahoma Press, 1957) provides a detailed account of the adoption of the Amendments.

Collections of documents and cases abound. However, two such efforts are particularly useful. These are Chafee's broadranging *Documents on Fundamental Human Rights** (New York: Atheneum Publishers, 1963) and Levy's collection *Freedom of the Press from Zenger to Jefferson** (Indianapolis: The Bobbs-Merrill Co., Inc., 1966) which includes early essay material often difficult to obtain in smaller libraries. A similar collection in the same series (edited by Levy), Harold Nelson's *Freedom of the Press from Hamilton to the Warren Court** (Indianapolis: The Bobbs-Merrill Co., Inc., 1967) is judiciously chosen and edited.

The fullest collection of legal materials is Thomas Emer-

---

1. Titles marked with an asterisk are available in paperback.

son, David Haber, and Norman Dorsen, *Political and Civil Rights in the United States* (3rd ed. Boston: Little, Brown and Co., 1967). Appropriate sections of the *Constitution of the United States of America, analysis and interpretation* (Washington: U.S. Government Printing Office, 1964) are useful short treatments. Corwin's editing of the 1952 volume made this a major reference work and the present editors have maintained the quality of the volume. Legalistic analysis of more recent events can be found in C. Herman Pritchett's *The Roosevelt Court* (New York: The Macmillan Company, 1948) and *The Political Offender and the Warren Court* (Boston: Boston University Press, 1958) as well as his magisterial *The American Constitution* (New York: McGraw-Hill Book Co., Inc., 1959).

Harry Kalven's *The Negro and the First Amendment** (Chicago: University of Chicago Press, 1966) is a work of great verve and subtlety which illuminates all aspects of its subject matter. Martin Shapiro has marshaled the case for preferred freedom in his *Freedom of Speech** (Englewood Cliffs: Spectrum Books, 1966), while Alexander Meiklejohn's *Political Freedom** (New York: Galaxy Books, 1965) is the classic exposition of absolutism. The views of Black, Brennan, and other Justices are conveniently pinpointed in their own public lectures assembled by Edmond Cahn (ed.) *The Great Rights* (New York, New York University Press, 1963).

An unconventional, though now somewhat outdated critique of classic liberal views of free speech is Walter Berns' *Freedom, Virtue and the First Amendment* (Baton Rouge: Louisiana State University Press, 1957). A more trenchent discussion, though often marred by irrelevent *ad hominem* discourses, is found in the scattered essays of Willmoore Kendall; some of the better and fuller treatments are collected in his *The Conservative Affirmation* (Chicago: Henry Regnery Co., 1963). A statement of a more complex position—generally libertarian but excepting totalitarians from tolerance—is found *inter alia* in Sidney Hook *Heresy, Yes, Conspiracy, No* (New York: John Day Co., 1963).

The most important work on public opinion and liberty remains Samuel Stouffer's much criticized and influential *Communism, Conformity and Civil Liberties* (New York: Doubleday and Co., Inc., 1955). Walter Murphy and Joseph Tanenhaus have been engaged in a venturesome study of public opinion and the Supreme Court. Unfortunately, the first fruits of this, still in the form of a preliminary paper, had barely become available as this book went to press. Current behavioral research on the courts is well represented in Glendon Schubert (ed.) *Judicial Behavior* (Chicago: Rand McNally and Co., 1964) and in the forthcoming volume of the proceedings of the Shambaugh Conference (University of Iowa, October 1967). Much of the material is summarized in Schubert's *The Judicial Mind* (Evanston: Northwestern University Press, 1965) and in Samuel Krislov *The Supreme Court and the Political Process* (New York: The Macmillan Company, 1965). Christian Bay's *The Structure of Freedom**
(New York: Atheneum Publishers, 1965) is a classic attempt to define the psychological matrix of freedom. Lucius and Twiley Barker, Jr., *Freedoms, Courts, Publics* (Englewood Cliffs: Prentice-Hall, Inc., 1965), attempt to explain the social matrix of selected court decisions.

The literature on the proper role of the court is seemingly endless. For recent discussions the student should consult Charles Black's *The People and the Court* (New York: The Macmillan Company, 1960), Learned Hand's *The Bill of Rights* (Cambridge: Harvard University Press, 1958) and Alexander Bickel's *The Least Dangerous Branch* (Indianapolis: The Bobbs-Merrill Co., Inc., 1962). The most sensitive discussions are Herbert Wechsler's influential—if somewhat delphic—*Principles, Politics and Fundamental Law* (Cambridge: Harvard University Press, 1961) and Gearld Gunther's quietly profound "The Subtle Vices and the Passive Virtues," (*64 Columbia Law Review*, 1, 1964).

Table of Cases

Index